‖‖‖‖‖ ‖‖‖‖‖‖‖‖‖‖‖‖‖‖‖‖‖
I0085337

Inviting Nature to Dinner

The benefits of bringing biodiversity to our backyards

Preview version

by Helen Schwencke and Dick Copeman

We respectfully acknowledge the
First Australians, the Aboriginal and Torres Strait Islander peoples,
for their stewardship of the country and its plants and animals,
for the strength and durability of their culture and
for the heritage of bush foods that they have shared with us,
the more recent inhabitants of this land.

Earthling Enterprises

2020

© **2020** Helen Schwencke and Dick Copeman, Earthling Enterprises

Published by:
Earthling Enterprises Pty. Ltd.,
ABN: 81 050 5 919
PO Box 5167, West End, Qld, Australia 4101
Internet: www.earthling.com.au
Email: info@earthling.com.au

ISBN 978-0-9757138-2-2

A catalogue record for this work is available from the National Library of Australia

Credits
The photos are used with permission and are copyright to:
Helen Schwencke, Dick Copeman, Annette Faith Dexter, Frank Jordan, Glenn Leiper, Teale Britstra, Ute Harder de Sohnrey, Amelia Pasieczny, Erica Siegel, Stephen Noble, Beth Cavallari, Chris Schwencke, Shanna Bignell, Jacob Krijt, Rob Macaulay, Todd Burrows, Trish Gardner, Christina Yeomans

Book production and publication by Helen Schwencke

Cover design
Helen Schwencke and Amelia Pasieczny

The front cover shows the lifecycle of the Chequered Swallowtail butterfly (*Papilio demoleus*), early and late stage caterpillars, chrysalis, and the upper and underside wings of the adult, a female butterfly laying an egg (Christina Yeomans), along with its host plant, Emu Foot (*Cullen tenax*). Also shown is a Round Lime (*Citrus australis*) branch with fruit, showing an Orchard Swallowtail caterpillar and a female Orchard Swallowtail butterfly.

The back cover shows: Centre - a Garden Mantis (*Orthodera ministralis*) with a firm hold on its caterpillar meal (Chris Schwencke). Clockwise from top left - a Common Assassin Bug nymph (*Pristhesancus plagipennis*) eating an Australian Leafroller Tachinid Fly (most likely a *Trigonospila cingulata*) (Annette Dexter); a Northern Green Jumping Spider (*Mopus mormon*) stalking its next meal, a nymph hemipteran bug (Helen Schwencke); a newly hatched Common Assassin Bug nymph, with its sibling unhatched eggs nearby, eating an aphid; a Ladybird larva eating an aphid parasitised by a wasp; a Hover Fly larva eating an aphid (all Chris Schwencke).

Illustrations:
p. 9   Tree of living organisms, illustrated by Maulucioni y Doridí (2013), licensed
         under the Creative Commons Attribution-Share Alike 3.0. Unported license.
p. 11 Insects relative to all other animals: Helen Schwencke & Amelia Pasieczny
p. 11 Species scape: Clint Penick & Magdalena Sorger, used with permission
p. 17 Food web: Paula Peeters

Lifecycle illustrations throughout the text are based on Helen's extensive series called Butterfly Lives: lifecycle and ecology interpretation signs, available via:
www.earthling.com.au/butterfly-lives/

Typesetting:
Text: NimbusRomanNo9, Heading: Arial, Header: InkFree, Captions: Liberation Serif

How to use this book

This book is really an invitation to come on a journey - a journey of exploring how we can work with nature, especially the small creatures in nature, to live sustainably while stewarding the land and enabling as much biodiversity to co-exist with us as possible in our little patches on this beautiful Earth. In the pages that follow, we offer a whole new perspective on gardening.

We are taking an unusual approach with the initial version of this book: we are inviting your discussion and feedback. In order to be certain that we are meeting your needs and interests, we are asking you to let us know what you think of it. Consider it as a pilot or beta version. The information contained in the book is in no way complete or all encompassing at this stage, nor are there as many images as will be in the next version.

Rather than working in a bubble of our own, creating something we hope is informative and useful, based on what we, the authors, think would be good for you to know, our intention is to have a discussion with you to help develop further editions of a book that is really useful to a wider audience.

To connect with us and give us feedback, please use one or other of the following channels:

- Email your comments to info@earthling.com.au

- Join the Facebook page: Inviting Nature to Dinner

- Post discussion comments to your own Facebook page and tag @Helen Schwencke If you use platforms other than Facebook and would like to engage with us, please let us know.

- Join the Earthling Enterprises mailing list to receive very occasional emails about events or discussions about the contents of this publication and others relating to how we interact with insects and other invertebrates: http://eepurl.com/gvLH2n.

We invite you to post your own observations and photos, when you're gardening with nature, in line with the ideas presented here. Please post these to your own pages and/or to the Facebook sites above, or email them to us.

If you would like some prompts for giving us feedback, please see the Conclusion.

We will use your feedback to inform the next version, which we aim to produce within twelve months.

Acknowledgments

Helen

We all stand on the shoulders of many giants, enabling us to see a bit more of a bigger picture. In naming names I would need to leave out more people whose work has informed this effort than can possibly be included.

The giants in the field of biology and ecology are there for all to see in the literature. Likewise those in the field of natural history, initially, and subsequently various specialties such as entomology, and more specifically those who have specialised in groups such as the Lepidoptera, butterflies and moths, which first piqued my curiosity about plant-eating insects, are also due their recognition. Then there's the many who have played huge roles in landscape designing, gardening, permaculture and farming.

The people who have influenced this work the most directly have been those involved with the Butterfly and Other Invertebrates Club, and the Queensland Naturalists' Club. Alongside that, is the pleasure of the hundreds of conversations I've had, since 2003, at the Woodford Folk Festival with my active involvement with its Butterfly and other Invertebrates Project at the festival itself, and at the monthly Treehugger and Butterfly working bees.

The first person who I'd like to directly acknowledge by name is Dick Copeman, my co-author. Without Dick's insights and knowledge about gardening and permaculture, his input and questions, our lengthy discussions, his considerable writing skills, and great ability to keep us on track, this book may have taken much longer to take form. Many thanks to you Dick.

The second person is my daughter, Amelia, for her deep and amazing nature observation and interpretation ability, and for her way with words.

Dick

I embarked on this project with Helen because of my interest in growing plants for food, for which I owe much to my colleagues at Northey Street City Farm in Brisbane over the past 26 years, including in particular, John Morahan, Tash Morton, Tim Lang, Bunya Halasz and Ko Oishi. Annette McFarlane was a valued teacher and mentor in the early years at the city farm.

My interest in native plants developed from my involvement in bush revegetation projects with colleagues including Jenny Leask, Fran Thomas and Tali Shelley, and has continued to develop with the support of members of the Queensland Naturalists' Club and of my long-standing friend, Ron Carr. My interest in bush foods was sparked by John Wrench and nurtured by him and other members of the Queensland Bushfood Association.

When I had to teach about 'pests and diseases' in a permaculture course at the city farm, Adrian Holbeck, helped me observe the myriad of little 'critters' at the farm and understand the ways in which they interacted with the crops and other plants. Later, Helen, John Moss and Peter Woodall from the Naturalists' Club helped me identify insects and learn about their life cycles and relationships.

The teachings and writings of David Holmgren and Dave Jacke inspired me to look closely at the ecology of gardening and Michael Wardle helped me clarify my approach to applying their ideas.

The passion of my co-author, Helen, for this topic has inspired a similar passion in me, which has helped me expand my understanding of invertebrates and their significance in the overall scheme of things, particularly in their relationships with plants.

Finally, my partner, Helen Abrahams, has, as always, been generous with her support and her love.

Table of Contents

1. Why this book?

We have a good news story which we hope will surprise and delight you.

However, in the offering of it, we do need to dip into some bad news along the way.

We can all start making a big difference for our local environment, by taking small steps in our gardens, steps such as providing food sources for butterflies and other small creatures, especially their larval forms, by growing their local native host plants. Not only will we experience the joy and delight of having these colourful creatures in our garden but we will also be supporting them to play their individual roles in the whole web of life that, in turn, will support creatures such as birds, frogs, lizards and many others. In the process they will also support the other plants in our gardens. How? That is the story of this book - how to garden with nature.

There is no "one size fits all" when it comes to gardening. There's even less of a "one size fits all" when it comes to gardening with nature, that is using ecological principles. Every place is different. While the core

To take good advantage of what we're offering as a discussion starter, it will help immensely if you have grounding in the basic principles of Ecology. There are some great, short and pithy, online courses on the topic. The Khan Academy has a beautifully presented very short online course which can be found at: https://www.khanacademy.org/science/biology/ecology/intro -to-ecology/v/ecology- introduction.

principles themselves are widely applicable, the specifics of how they work in any situation are completely dependent on that garden, landscape, soil type and ecosystem.

Much of the gardening advice, using the "one size fits all" approach, tells us to isolate the plants we want for our own use. Isolating food plants doesn't take into account ecological principles and as a result requires high levels of maintenance and attention. Isolated plants in bare ground (or mulch) may as well have a flag planted beside them that says "come and eat me". The pesticides, fertilisers, tillage and irrigation required to produce food this way means that our farming systems use many times more energy than they produce in food, while poisoning and degrading the soil as well. This is completely unsustainable.

To make our food production sustainable, we need firstly to understand that all life on earth lives in complex relationships with other life and the environment, in a highly interdependent way. We then need to adjust the way we garden and grow our food so that we are working with, not against, nature and its complex relationships.

Several key facts underpin the case we make in this book. Over two thirds of all animal species are insects, of which around a third are herbivores or plant eaters.This is in the little-known context that 95 out of every 100 of all the described animal species on Earth are invertebrates, that is, creatures without backbones, which include insects. Each species has its own role to play and the roles and the species are not interchangeable. Terrestrial life on Earth is dependent firstly on sunlight providing energy for plants to produce carbohydrates and then on herbivores, mostly insects[17], converting the carbohydrates to proteins. These protein rich herbivores are, in turn,

vital food for other animals, particularly their young. Finally, only a very small proportion of insects and other invertebrate species have any negative impact on people or
on the plants and animals we favour and nurture.

The concepts discussed in this book are relevant to all biogregions; however the specific examples used in this discussion are relevant to the bioregion known as the
Macleay-McPherson Overlap, particularly the coastal part of this bioregion on the
east coast of Australia between roughly Noosa and Coffs Harbour. This is where the
subtropical and temperate climatic zones overlap and it is a very biodiverse bioregion,
with, for example, 200 of Australia's 400 butterflies and similarly diverse populations
of plants and other animals.

As you begin to appreciate some of nature's complex relationships, and to see what a
huge difference replacing ornamental garden plants with local native plants makes to
the species richness in your garden and neighbourhood, you will, like us, be wanting
to share your excitement with your neighbours and fellow gardeners. Our shared
small steps will, as others follow our example and invite nature to dinner, become
one giant leap for our environment and all the organisms we share it with.

Decline of insects and other invertebrates

Entomologists and ecologists have been reporting for some years that insect numbers
have been declining. In 2006, researchers reported dramatic declines in counts of
moths attracted to light traps in Great Britain[1] while a 2010 international gathering of
firefly experts reported downward trends in their numbers worldwide[2]. Entomologists
in Australia noticed on their drives through the countryside that they were no longer
having to clean the dead insects off the windscreens of their cars[3]. A 2014 summary
of global declines in biodiversity and abundance estimated a 45 percent drop in the
abundance of invertebrates, most of which are insects[4].

In 2017, more definitive evidence came from a study in Germany where amateur
entomologists had been collecting insects in standard traps across 63 nature areas
since 1989. The weight of the insects caught in each sample was measured and anal-
ysed and revealed that the annual average weight of insects found in the traps fell by
76% over the 27-year period of their research[39]. Another German study found clear
evidence of substantial declines in arthropod abundance and biodiversity. In grasslands, species richness of arthropods fell by 34% over a ten year period, and the arthropod biomass and numbers recorded dropped by 67% and 78%, respectively. These
declines were particularly strong in landscapes dominated by farmland, suggesting
that agricultural management could be driving this drop. The losses among forest-
dwelling arthropods were less precipitous.[5]

A 2018 report of a study from Puerto Rica showed that the mass of arthropods
(insects and spiders) in a rainforest reserve decreased by at least three quarters from
1976 to 2013[6], while a 2018 census found a marked drop in monarch butterflies along
the California coast[7]. Many other individual species and species groups are declining
or even being threatened with extinction, from bumblebees in Europe[8] and the

United States[9] to fungus weevils in Africa[10]. A recent meta-analysis of 166 long-term surveys of insect occurence in many parts of the world found an average decline of terrestrial insect abundance by about 9% per decade, although freshwater insect abundance increased by about 11% per decade[38].

There are a whole range of possible reasons for the decline of insects, the details of which are still being worked out by entomologists and ecologists. However, it is becoming clear that the main causes of their decline are that their habitat has been destroyed, that they have been poisoned by pesticides and other chemicals, that invasive species and new diseases are displacing and killing them and that climate change is altering the environmental conditions they have evolved to live in[3].

Habitat destruction

Habitat loss is the most insidious of all threats facing land-living wildlife. Habitat is being lost through land clearing for grazing and farming, which continues, both on a broad scale, and also through enlargement of farm fields, with loss of remnant native plants on the edges of the fields. Also, as cities get bigger, the bush on their expanding edges is bulldozed, and the ground scraped bare and remodelled for houses. Green belts are taken over by invasive plants, roads and infrastructure.

Chemicals

Pesticides are specifically designed to kill insects directly and their usage has increased in Australia from the 1990s. However, there is very little data available on pesticide use and environmental impact in this country, which makes it difficult to judge how our flora and fauna are responding to continued exposure to these toxins.

It is estimated that 70% of the world's native bee species are earth dwelling and that there are at least 2,000 native bee species in Australia. All cicada species have nymph stages that live in the soil. 350 Australian species have been identified so far, with many more anticipated. As land is bull-dozed and reshaped for housing, industrial, agricultural, and other development, and this spreads further and further across the landscape, perhaps you can begin to imagine the impact of this practice on insect species declines at least at local levels.

Overseas, reports linking the decline of both honeybee and wild bee populations in Europe to exposure to neonicotinoid insecticides has led the EU to ban neonicotinoid use except in greenhouses. At the time of writing, Australian authorities are reviewing neonicotinoid use here.

It is not just pesticides that are of concern. All up, there are 100,000+ artificial chemicals registered for use globally in industry and elsewhere, with more than 30,000 produced in commercial quantities[11]. Only one in seven of these have been adequately assessed for their environmental safety while one in five have not been assessed at all[11]. Some of them inevitably end up in the environment, with unknown, but potentially serious impacts on wildlife, including insects.

*Two images of ground covers at Moggill Conservation Park, off Mt Crosby Rd, taken after a long dry spell. Top image shows the introduced Creeping lantana (**Lantana montevidensis**) blanketing out habitat for other, native, species. The bottom image is from a location within 20m, "messier" though showing diverse native plant species (at least 5 species) and in a smaller area than the top photo.*
Helen Schwencke, May 2020

Invasive species

As an island nation, Australia's unique flora and fauna is particularly prone to disruption by invasive species. Not only do they directly kill native species but their lack of natural predators also allows these introduced species to flourish and take over the living space and food resources of the native species. While the cane toad, rabbit, fox and cat are well known invasive species, local native insects are also being threatened by invasive plants and invasive insects.

Invasive plants displace the native plants that are host and food plants for native insects, but support far fewer insects themselves. Invasive insects compete with and displace local insects, transmit new diseases to them and disrupt pollination of native plants.

Climate change

Climate change is altering the timing of flowering and fruiting of plants and is causing a range of other effects. With increasing carbon dioxide in the air, plants are growing faster but they are less nutritious, and they also have more energy to commit to their defences against being eaten by insects. Insects are also being affected as heat waves have been shown to make the males of some species less fertile.

Some experts have called this decline an "insect armageddon", while another has predicted that 40% of insects are threatened with extinction if the current rate of decline continues[3]. The seemingly rapid and marked decline in insects, if it is confirmed globally, will have grave consequences for all life on earth, as we will elaborate later. The distinguished Harvard biologist Edward O Wilson summed it up nicely when he observed that insects are "the little things that run the world" and that "If all humankind were to disappear, the world would regenerate back to the rich state of equilibrium that existed 10,000 years ago. If insects were to vanish, the environment would collapse into chaos." However, there are always winners and losers in any ecological change.

Ecological simplification

While the extinction of one life-form frequently leads to the loss of other life forms, it can also open up habitat for some lifeforms, usually those species that are generalists, and often those that are invasive. So, while the number of species is declining, the abundance of a small number of species is increasing; these are all adaptable, generalist species that are occupying the vacant niches left by the ones declining [3].

Our own houses and gardens in cities are a good example. Unless some effort for including nature has been made, they are almost scorched earth from a diversity point of view. The creatures that live with us quite happily, such as introduced rats, cockroaches, mice, silverfish and, more recently, Asian barking geckoes, are mostly creatures that can use the resources our lives make available. And many gardens, especially if they comprise non-native plants including grasses, are great habitat for a native generalist grasshopper, green-headed ants that bite painfully, lawn grubs, and a small range of moth caterpillars that eat the plants we nurture.

Thus the winners from the decline of insect species are likely to be creatures that we don't want to share our lives with, potentially resulting in higher levels of use of chemicals to control them. The core problem resulting from our human actions, often unintended, is that we have created simpler and simpler ecosystems. This process of simplifying an ecosystem or habitat creates what are called vacant or empty niches. The implications of this for our gardens will be described in more detail in Section 3, The ecology of growing our food.

A helpful explanation about how nature works can be found in a book by Douglas Tallamy "Bringing Nature Home"[12]

While the likely causes of the insect decline may seem to be beyond our influence as individuals, that is not the case. This is our chance to start increasing the complexity of the ecosystems in our local spaces and places. We can make a significant contribution to bringing nature back into our urban areas and gardens by doing some simple things in the local places and spaces that we can influence and control directly.

A role for gardeners

As gardeners, we pride ourselves in taking good care of the plants we grow in our small patch of earth. We don't always realise, however, that it is not just us, but many other creatures, that also depend on our plant to satisfy their needs. We also don't always realise that the choices and decisions that we make about what plants to grow, how to nurture them and how to manage our garden spaces can have life and death implications for these creatures and others dependent on them.

Like all living creatures, insects, other invertebrates and other smaller animals need water, shelter, space, their own specific food and an appropriate environment. If we re-create the habitats that provide these needs in our gardens, we will help ensure that these smaller creatures are able to survive and thrive and return to playing their important roles in the web of life.

Supporting these diverse creatures will also support our efforts to grow our preferred plants by working with nature as an ally. Re-creating as much of a complex web of life within our gardens as possible provides a population of predator species that are on hand to help control outbreaks of 'pest' or competitor species.

With the continuing decline in the amount and quality of native bushland, our home and community gardens become more important as places that can provide the biodiversity of local native plants required to support our native wildlife, especially invertebrates and other small animals. As gardeners, we can play a key role and set an example for other gardeners and land carers so that together we can ensure the survival of these vital little critters.

We hope that the pages that follow will both inspire you to become a backyard biodiversity builder and also give you some tools with which to begin.

2. The diversity of life - why every species counts

The plants, animals, fungi and microbes on earth have evolved by interacting with each other and the environment over many millennia to create an amazing array, or **biodiversity**, of different species. Species interact with other species in different ways, some competing and others supporting, some eating others, and others being eaten. Each species requires a unique set of environmental conditions for it to survive and reproduce and also plays a unique role within the whole **ecosystem** of interacting organisms and environments.

The various ecosystems in Australia, including sclerophyll forests, rainforests, heath-lands, grasslands, etc., all comprise different communities of plants, animals and microbes. When we as humans first encounter a particular natural ecosystem, we tend to assume that it is permanent and unchanging, that each plant or animal is happily fulfilling its own role and main-taining its own stable population. We often don't realise that ecosystems are not static, that all ecosystems are subject to periodic disturbance by storm, flood, drought and fire, and that these disturbances cause ebbs and flows in the populations of all living organisms.

At one time you'll have a Casuarina forested gully in Toohey Forest that becomes known as a egular overwintering site for Common Crow butterflies. Upon revisiting it 20 years later it's an open Brushbox forest

As ecosystems change in response to disturbance, their biodiversity is the key to how well they can survive and recover from the disturbance. An ecosystem with greater biodiversity has more organisms fulfilling more roles, but also more overlap between these roles. The organisms are adapted to a wider range of environmental conditions, and there are more interactions between organisms. So when a more biodiverse ecosystem is disturbed and the numbers of some species, or their population sizes, are reduced, it is more likely that others will be able to take over parts of their roles or adjust to the changed environmental conditions. Ecosystems with less biodiversity are less able to adjust to and recover from disturbance and if the disturbance is large or continuing, they may become permanently degraded and unable to support much biodiversity.

Protecting and supporting biodiversity is thus essential for maintaining the resilience of ecosystems. Resilient, healthy ecosystems serve important functions on which all life depends - cleaning air, purifying water, recycling waste, cycling nutrients, mod-erating weather and pollinating food crops. When a species becomes extinct. all the other lifeforms that are associated with it have their viability affected, biodiversity declines, ecosystems become less resilient and the environment is degraded.

We may enjoy the colour and movement of butterflies or the patterns their caterpillars make on plant leaves, we may love to watch a praying mantis stalking its prey, a spider rushing in to consume an insect trapped in its web or a dragonfly hovering over water, and we may be intrigued as our ears pick up the loud buzz of a carpenter bee pollinating flowers. For many of us, the emotions that insects and other invertebrates awaken in us may make us want to act to help ensure that they survive and thrive and are protected from threats to their survival mentioned elsewhere.

However, for many, an even more powerful motivation to act to support and protect all species comes when we recognise that all life forms play a role in maintaining biodiversity and that the loss of even one species, no matter how small or seemingly insignificant, weakens the ecosystem of which it is a part. The more species that are lost, the greater is the impact on the ecosystem.

Overview of life-forms, classification, life cycles, behaviour and ecology.

Why is it important for us as gardeners to consider the whole range of life on Earth?

Just because we can't see it, it doesn't mean it's not there - our human perception misses many things. If we don't have a concept of the full scope of life, we inevitably and unknowingly end up making decisions that affect other life-forms badly, even those life forms that are our greatest allies.

If you'd like to review the basic of taxonomy and how life on earth is classified then the Khan Academy taxonomy topic **Taxonomy and The Tree of Life** *is well presented: https://www.khanacademy.org/science/high-school-biology/hs-evolution/hs-phylogeny/v taxonomy-and-the-tree-of-life*

Our decisions about what lives and dies, no matter how small those decisions are, when they are aggregated across the whole human population, now have a significant impact on all life on Earth. Once we understand the full scope of life on earth, however, we will start making different decisions, decisions that will support, not diminish, all life forms and their amazing biodiversity.

Life-forms on Earth - how they are classified

It is a long-held understanding of biologists that life-forms on Earth evolved from simple organisms that, over many millennia, gradually evolved to become more complex, leading to the diversity of life-forms we can now observe.

Current thinking is that this diversity of life-forms can be grouped into two domains, comprising seven kingdoms. For the sake of simplicity, we are using a Tree of Life diagram (opposite) that shows six groupings of these life forms within these two domains:

Prokaryota
- single-celled organisms with no defined nucleus, comprising the kingdoms of:

- Bacteria
- Archaea

Eukaryota

- all other organisms, which have cells containing distinct organ-elles, including a nucleus (which contains the genetic material) surrounded by a membrane. They comprise the following Kingdoms:

- **Protista**, which is now differentiated into two kingdoms:

  - **Protozoa**
    - some single-celled animals formerly in Protista

  - **Chromista**
    - single and multicellular organisms with organelles called

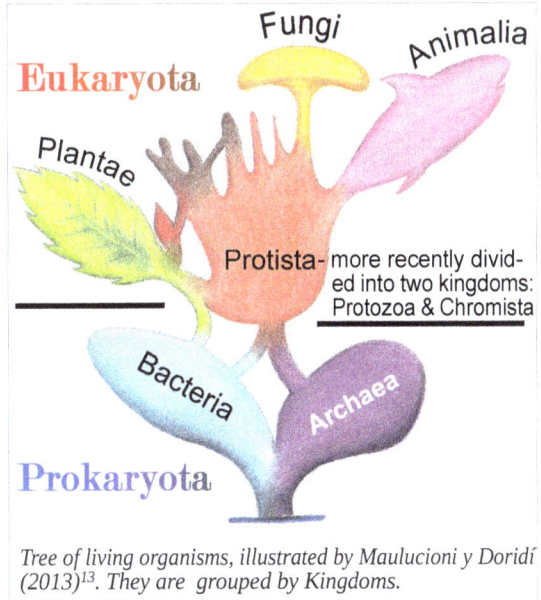

Tree of living organisms, illustrated by Maulucioni y Doridí (2013)[13]. They are grouped by Kingdoms.

plastids which contain chlorophyll c. These include algae, diatoms, oomycetes, and some other protozoans, with plastids, formerly in Protista

- **Fungi**
  - including mushrooms, yeasts and moulds - organisms with chitin in their cell wall, something they share with animals to which they are more closely related than plants. Like animals, they also ingest food as their source of energy.

- **Plantae** (Plants)
  - with cellulose-based cell walls and organelles called chloroplasts that use solar energy, water and carbon dioxide from the air to produce carbohydrates through the process of photosynthesis.

- **Animalia** (Animals)
  - mobile organisms that consume organic material as food, breathe oxygen, reproduce sexually and develop from an embryo that is a hollow sphere of cells or blastula.

All living organisms are classified using a system developed by a Swedish scientist, Carl Linnaeus, in the 1730s, which developed as a field that came to be known as taxonomy. Within each Kingdom, each individual species is scientifically classified and described according to the other life-forms it is most closely related to. At each level in this classification system the life-forms grouped together share a specific set of characteristics.

So, to take an Australian insect, the Lemon Migrant butterfly, as an example, it is catalogued as being in the:

Domain: **Eukaryota**

Kingdom: **Animalia**

Phylum: **Arthropoda** - a large group of animals, including crabs and spiders that have "jointed legs". This is one of the 33 Phyla collectively called Invertebrates.

Class: **Insecta** - Arthropoda that have 6 legs, including ants, bees, crickets, beetles, flies and many more

Order: **Lepidoptera** - Insecta with scale-covered wings, namely butterflies and moths.

Family: **Pieridae** - a group of Lepidoptera, which are commonly called the Whites and Yellows.

Genus: *Catopsilia*

Species: *Catopsilia pomona*, as illustrated here.

*Lemon Migrant (**Catopsilia pomona**) Helen Schwencke*

So-called common names such as Lemon Migrant can be different in different places, or used for more than one species, which is why using scientific names is important, so we can reasonably assume we are all talking about the same life-form.

The diversity of life

Each of the Kingdoms of Life comprises from thousands up to millions of species. There are many different ways to represent all these species and their relationships to each other, and there is debate about which ones are the most accurate.

*Exploring various "Tree of Life" representations is a great rabbit warren to explore. We quite like **the Evogeneao version** which you can access at: http://www.evogeneao. com/en*

Ecologically speaking, we assume that all life-forms are as important as each other, even though we have barely scratched the surface of knowing much about most of them. For our purposes, however, we are focusing mainly on the plants and animals, largely because we rely on these two kingdoms for our food and many other necessities of life.

This is not to downplay the important ecological roles played by the life-forms of other kingdoms. Fungi, for instance, play a critical role as decomposers and in nutrient cycling in soil and on dead plants and also provide an underground communication system between plants, especially in ecosystems where a wide variety of organisms present have co-evolved. Bacteria, likewise, are key players in nutrient digestion and disease control in many animals and plants, notwithstanding the fact that a very small number of them also cause diseases of plants and animals.

In the process of learning to live and let live, the five other groups of organisms that we don't focus on will be in a better position to thrive unimpeded and perform their roles, if we take a less interventionist approach, except perhaps where a small number of species are causing an actual problem with our food production.

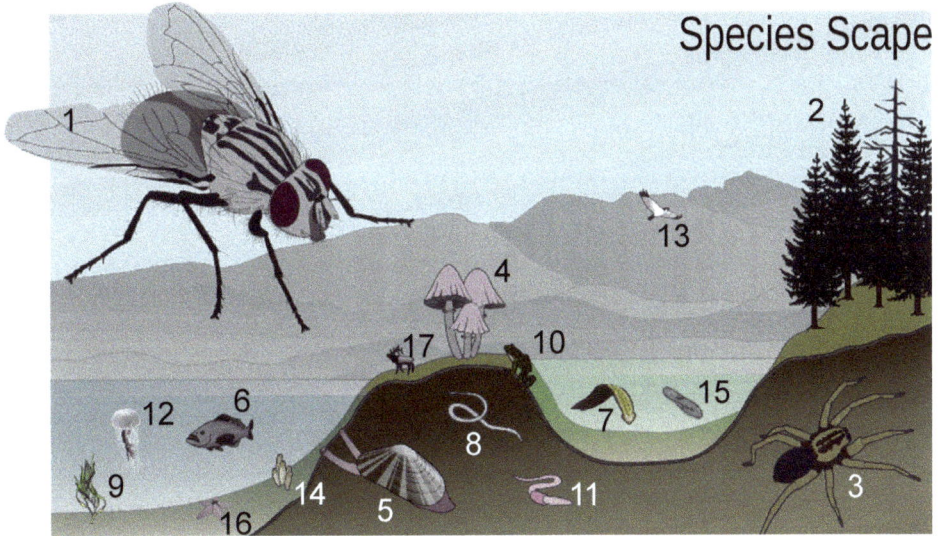

Species Scape

Legend

1. Insects	1,063587	7. Flatworms (Platyhelminthes)	29,487	11. Segmented worms (Annelida)	17,388
2. Plants	422,000	8. Roundworms (Nematoda)	25,033	12. Cnidarians	10,183
3. Non-insect arthropods	203,462	9. Chromista (Algae & allies)	17,892	13. Birds	10,055
4. Fungi	100,000			14. Sponges (Porifera)	8,659
5. Molluscs	84,077	10. Reptiles and Amphibians	17,892	15. Protozoa	8,118
6. Fish	32,834			16. Echinoderms	7,550
				17. Mammals	5,898

This simplified Species Scape shows the relative proportions of the number of species in each vertebrate and invertebrate group on the planet, along with plants, algae and fungi. Mammals, including humans are represented by the tiny elk, insects by the large fly. Only those Phyla with over 5,000 species are included. Illustration by by Clint Penick & Magdalena Sorger, after Quentin Wheeler (1990)[14].

Insects relative to all other animals

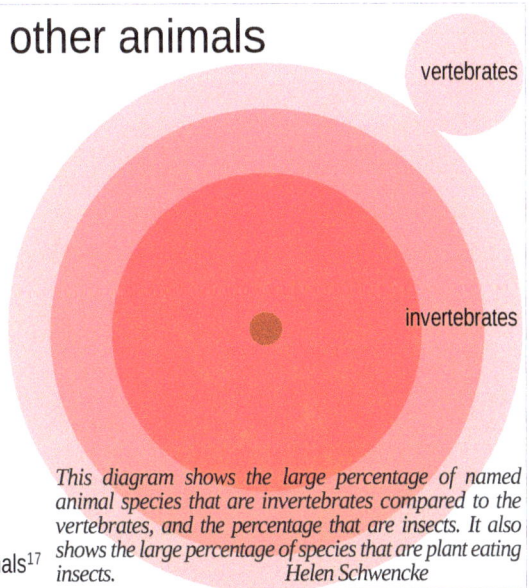

vertebrates

All named animal species[15]

- vertebrates 5% (the smaller separate circle)
- invertebrates 95% (the larger circle)

Of which invertebrates

- insects comprise 67% of named animals

- plant eating insects comprise 34% of all named animals[15,17]

- insects that have "pest" potential comprise < 0.34% of all named animals[17]

invertebrates

This diagram shows the large percentage of named animal species that are invertebrates compared to the vertebrates, and the percentage that are insects. It also shows the large percentage of species that are plant eating insects.   Helen Schwencke

Within the animal kingdom, most of the vertebrates (animals with backbones) have been described and classified but the task of estimating the numbers of inverte-brates (animals without backbones) is still a very long way from complete. There are 72,478 vertebrates known to science, and approximately 1.5M invertebrates have been described[10].

In the Species Scape illustration on the previous page, you can see from the size of the fly relative to that of all other creatures depicted that, there are many more insect species than all other animal species put together. They comprise at least two-thirds of invertebrate species[15] and probably more, as estimates for the total number of insect species on earth vary between 3M and 12M[16]. Another way of stating these proportions is that, at the present state of play, 95 out of 100 of the identified animal species on the planet are invertebrates, and at least 67 of them are insects.

Another way of representing these proportions is the "Insects relative to all other animals" diagram on page 11. This also shows the proportion of insects that are herbivorous (plant eaters), the significance of which will be discussed in the next section.

Insect diversity

Over their 400 million year period of evolution, insects have diversified into millions of species that occupy virtually every corner of the land and freshwater environments on earth. To understand the different roles that insects play, it helps to have some understanding of the way that they are classified and grouped. They are divided into 29 groups or Orders whose members have common features.

Of those 67 insects out of 100 animals mentioned earlier, around 34 are insect herb-ivores or plant eaters, that is, approximately 51 out of every 100 invertebrates is a herb-ivorous insect[17]. If you take a moment to think about this, there are a staggering num-ber of insect herbivores, and that number includes only those that have been identi-fied so far.

Butterflies, by way of example, are insect herbivores, as their caterpillars eat the leaves, flowers, fruit and/or seeds of plants, while the adult butterflies eat nectar and pollen from the flowers of plants. The food plants for butterfly caterpillars are best known of all the insects and are therefore a great starting place for food gardens where you want to enhance biodiversity.

Insect life cycles

In order to understand the roles that insects play, we need to know a bit about their life cycles. All insects change or "metamorphose" through several different stages, sometimes into very different looking animals, sometimes not. The different life stages often have different ecological roles, as we will see later.

Some insects hatch from the egg as nymphs, smaller versions of the adult insects, which then grow through a series of moults until they reach sexual maturity. This incomplete form of metamorphosis is used by grasshoppers, stick insects and cockroaches.

Butterflies and moths, saw-flies, bees, ants and wasps, beetles, lacewings, fleas and flies, on the other hand, undergo complete metamorphosis. They start as an egg, hatch into a larva, be it a caterpillar, grub or maggot, then change into an immobile pupa before finally emerging as an adult, ready to mate and reproduce. This process, which has only recently been documented, is utterly amazing.

What's going on inside the pupa while it's transitioning to the adult form?
Check out:
1. 3-D Scans Reveal Caterpillars Turning Into Butterflies
https://www.nationalgeographic.com/science/phenomena/2013/05/14/3-d-scans-caterpillars-transforming-butterflies-metamorphosis/
2. Imaginal discs
https://www.cell.com/current-biology/pdf/S0960-9822(10)00291-5.pdf

Common Crow butterfly - egg hatching

Left to right, top to bottom: 1st two rows: Common Crow butterfly mature egg hatching; 3rd row: newly hatched caterpillar making its first meal of the egg shell, and a one-day old caterpillar.   Helen Schwencke

Common Crow butterfly - caterpillar growing,moulting and pupating

Left to right, top to bottom: 1st row: first instar caterpillar with shed skin, 2nd instar caterpillar; 2nd and 3rd rows: caterpillar moulting then eating the shedded skin, and a caterpillar eating a leaf, 4th row: caterpillar preparing to pupate to become a pupa or chrysalis.   *Helen Schwencke*

Common Crow butterfly - chrysalis to butterfly emerging

Left to right, top to bottom: 1st row: chrysalis changing colour as the butterfly develops; 2nd and 3rd rows: butterfly emerging from pupal case and pumping up its wings; 4th row: open-winged adult butterfly, a mating pair, and a female, with abdomen curled, laying an egg

Helen Schwencke & Amelia Pasieczny

3. The ecology of growing our food

Plants

Imagine you are a big old tree in the back corner of your garden. The warm sun shines on your leaves, the cool rain falls through your canopy and seeps into the soil, and the gentle breeze blows all around you. Carbon dioxide from the air diffuses into your leaves where the energy from the sun helps combine it with water and minerals that have been pumped up from your roots, to form the sugars, starches and fibre that you need to grow your new shoots, roots, flowers and seeds.

As your roots grow into the soil, they team up with fungi to help you absorb the water and nutrients that you need to remain healthy. You pump thousands of litres of water each day up through your trunk and branches and out into the air, where it condenses to form clouds and rain.

It is cool and shady under your spreading branches and there are many nooks and crannies to provide homes and shelter for small creatures. They feast on your leaves, flowers, seeds and fruit, and their droppings enrich the soil that your roots feed from.

Their droppings also spread seeds into the soil where they sprout and form new plants. Under and around your canopy a whole new forest of plants, both big and small, grows and provides more shelter and food for all the small creatures that call your place home.

While the example above is a tree, all plant forms, sizes, shapes and growth habits are equally important - from ground covers, herbs and forbs, shorter and taller understorey plants to vines, scamblers, parasitic and hemi-parasitic plants, such as mistletoes - all have their essential and long-established roles to play.

In fact, when we discuss how to plan your wildlife friendly garden later in the book, you will see how important it is to include plants of all forms and sizes in your garden. And how important it is to understand what each plant's particular role is and what conditions each plant requires to flourish.

Food webs

The brief imagining that you are a tree underlines the fact that without plants there would be no life on earth as we know it. The sun's energy makes it possible for plants to produce carbohydrates as food for themselves. This then feeds every other living creature, largely through the huge number of insect species that eat plants, and in turn are eaten by other animals.

In ecological terms, plants are the producers on which consumers, including most living creatures, depend for their food and shelter. The ***producers*** and ***consumers*** together form a food web, as illustrated in the diagram opposite.

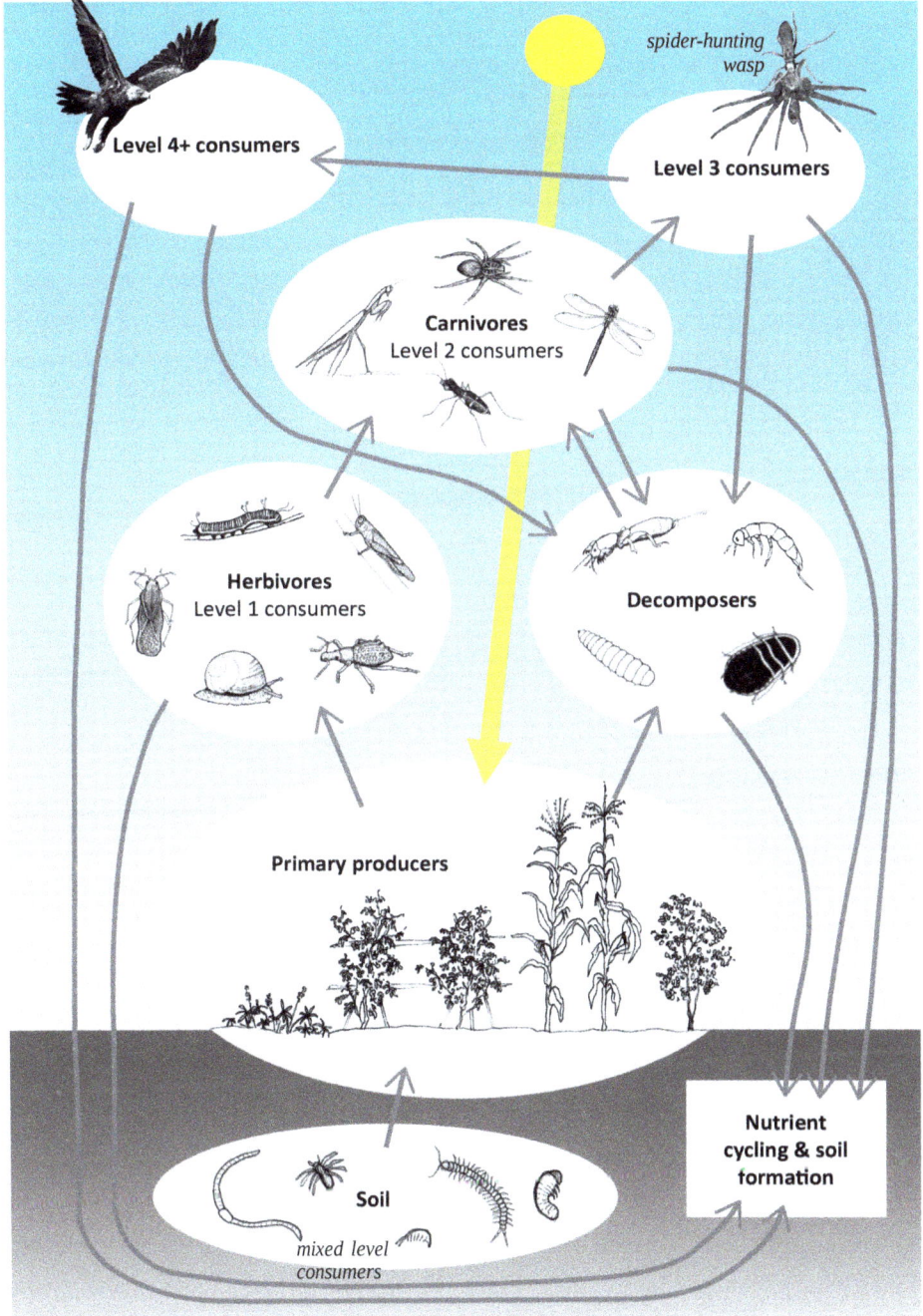

spider-hunting wasp

Level 4+ consumers

Level 3 consumers

Carnivores
Level 2 consumers

Herbivores
Level 1 consumers

Decomposers

Primary producers

Soil

mixed level
consumers

Nutrient
cycling & soil
formation

Food Web diagram: showing 'what eats what', and the movements of energy and nutrients in ecosystems. Plants (primary producers) use the energy of the sun to produce carbohydrates and store it in their living tissues. Herbivores (level 1 consumers) eat plants and are then eaten by carnivores (level 2 consumers). They, in turn are eaten by level 3 consumers, and so on. Decomposers eat dead organisms, and soil micro-organisms eat anything that's died and the droppings and waste from all the others and recycle their nutrients back to the plants.   *Illustration by Paula Peeters*

Insects

Insects are not only the major plant eaters or herbivores on the planet, even allowing for the huge numbers of domesticated mammalian herbivores such as cows, but they, with their close relatives, the Arachnids or spiders, also form the great majority of the level 2 consumers (see diagram p. 17). They also comprise a large portion of the decomposer species. Insects literally 'punch above their weight' in providing the work force that drives all ecological processes. Insects are able to serve all these functions because of their amazing diversity, as described earlier.

At least a third of all animal species, are insect herbivores, or plant eaters. Some herbivores, including the caterpillars of moths and butterflies, grasshoppers, weevils, leaf beetles, gall wasps, leaf-mining flies and plant bugs, eat the leaves, shoots or flowers of plants, while others, including adult butterflies and moths, aphids, scale insects, bees and hover flies, suck sap, nectar and pollen from plants.

You are probably aware of the role that many of these insects play as plant pollinators, transferring pollen from flower to flower to enable flowers to be fertilised and to develop into seeds and fruit. You may not be aware, however, that insect herbivores play another major, but largely unseen, role in maintaining healthy ecosystems. By eating young leaves and shoots, or scraping older leaves, they act as nature's pruners, controlling the growth of many plants, and by eating and excreting plant parts, they act as the forest's composters, digesting plant material and recycling nutrients back into the soil.

*Caterpillar of Speckled Line-blue butterfly (**Catopyrops florinda**) on Native mulberry (**Pipturus argenteus**), demonstrating its role of reducing leaf area, turning itself into a high protein package in the process and contributing to decomposition (those small black specks).*
Dick Copeman

The partially digested organic material in the insect droppings is further digested by the fungi and bacteria in the soil and converted into humus, the dark, spongy material that holds nutrients and water in the soil and releases them to plants as needed. Also, when plants lose a significant portion of their leaves, through herbivory, they shed a similar portion of their roots and these dead root fragments are then converted into humus in the soil. As the leaves grow back, so do the roots. Usually the plants survive and keep growing, but the net effect is that carbon is taken out of the atmosphere by the leaves, is then taken into the herbivorous insect and ends up being sequestered in the soil, thus helping reduce levels of greenhouse gas in the atmosphere.

Herbivorous insects are, in their turn, eaten by carnivorous insects, by other arthropods, such as spiders, and by a variety of creatures from other Phyla. These include some, such as dragonflies, damselflies, lacewings, beetles and mantids, that are predators, some of which directly hunt, while others lay in wait for their prey, grab it and eat it.

Other insects, such as fleas, mites, lice and mosquitoes, are micro-predators that bite and extract blood or other fluids from a prey animal. Another group, including some small wasps and Tachinid flies, are parasitoids that lay their eggs in or on prey such as caterpillars and aphids. The larvae that hatch from the eggs then feed on the prey insect internally and kill it in the process of using it as a source of food.

*An unidentified Tachinid fly (a parasitoid) stalking a Clearwing Swallowtail (**Cressida cressida**) caterpillar to attempt to lay eggs on it.   Helen Schwencke*

For some insects, their different life stages have different food requirements, with the larval or nymph stage being herbivorous while the adult stage is carnivorous, or vice versa. The larvae of most smaller wasps eat the flesh of other insects, while their adults eat only nectar from flowers. Lacewing larvae, also, are fierce carnivores while their adults may feed on nectar.

Allies and competitors

As gardeners, we know from bitter experience that when food plants are abundant and conditions are right, the populations of some herbivorous insects can increase rapidly so that they voraciously munch their way through our plants, eating the leaves we want, or the flowers and fruit. In this situation, these herbivores are our competitors for that food. However, if there are healthy populations of carnivorous insects nearby, they will start eating or parasitising the herbivores, which in turn will reduce the numbers of herbivores eating the plants. This also reduces the rate at which the competitor insect species population can increase. Having the reservoir of these allies nearby means that consumption of our preferred plants can be contained, allowing the food to be shared between the herbivores and us, the gardeners!

Gardening with nature in this way may require us to be a little more patient and to tolerate nibbled food plants. It also requires us to have a change of mindset from thinking of insects as either "pests" or "beneficials", or "baddies" or "goodies", to regarding them as "competitors" or "allies". Thinking ecologically in this way, we need to consider where the particular animal is at in its population cycle.

Thus we need to have populations of competitor animals, at least at a low level, to provide food to sustain the predator, parasitoid and disease allies that will kick in to reduce the competitor population when needed.

Many vertebrate animals also eat insects. Birds, reptiles and frogs, in particular, are dependent on good supplies of insects as high protein food. Even birds that eat mainly seeds or fruit as adults still rely on insects as the main food for their young. One of the reasons for the decline in many bird species is the decline in insect populations.

Population cycles

Every so often, we notice many more insects in our gardens than usual. Swarms of butterflies and moths are immediately obvious but, if we look closely, there will often be myriads of bees, wasps, beetles, bugs and other insects as well. These population explosions usually occur after a period of good summer rainfall that comes after a long spell of dry weather.

If you keep observing in the weeks after a population explosion starts, you will begin to notice that there are more spiders webs and that many of the caterpillars you find will have been parasitised, indicating that the numbers of the predators and parasitoid insects have increased, causing the populations of the next generation to crash.

During the dry period, the numbers of predators, parasites and diseases decrease and the numbers of active herbivorous insect species are also very low. When the rains come, the plants quickly put out flushes of new growth and vast numbers of different species of herbivorous insects, caterpillars and many others, are able to start eating and build up big populations very quickly, provided that they have populations nearby, or have populations of some dormant non-breeding part of their life cycle nearby. With few control agents around, for example, the 400 or so eggs that the females of many butterfly and moth species produce all have a better chance to complete their life cycles and go on to breed themselves, with each female laying another 400 or so eggs. The result can be a rapid, massive population explosion before the control species can get a look in.

There is another part to the story. Some insects have pupae that can go into a type of "suspended animation" called diapause in which the pupae don't finish metamorphosing immediately. Some species can stay in diapause for up to three years or perhaps even longer, waiting for conditions to become better before they complete their metamorphosis into the adult form.

These two mechanisms combined help explain how so many different species of herbivorous insects are able to build up populations so quickly and get a head start over their predators, parasitoids and diseases.

Plants and insects

Plants deploy a number of defences to discourage insects from eating them. Some contain chemicals that are toxic or distasteful to insects while others have leaves and other plant parts that are unpalatable because they are thick, hard, hairy or spiky. In many cases, a herbivore is able to eat a plant only when the leaves and shoots are young and tender, or if it has evolved to be able to cope with the particular defences that the plant uses. Each species of native herbivorous insect has evolved to be able to eat at least one species of native plant, which the insect depends on for its survival. In this case they are *specialist* feeders and will only live in an area that has those particular plants growing there. Other herbivores are *generalists* and will eat from a variety of plants.

Section 5, Case studies of native food plants that are also food for butterfly larvae, includes examples of butterflies and their specific host plants.

The evolution of plant defences and of a herbivore's ability to eat a plant happen in tandem and over many decades or centuries. On one side, the plant is continually trying to develop new defence strategies while on the other side, there is gradual selection of individual herbivores in succeeding generations, which can overcome or tolerate the plant's defences. This can eventually lead to the separation of a species into new and different species[18].

The time it takes for these evolutionary changes explains why native herbivorous insects are usually not able to eat exotic plants that are new or foreign to a particular area. They have not had sufficient time to adapt to the defences of the exotic plants they are encountering. Specialist insects, in particular, are rarely able to eat exotic plants, with some notable exceptions[19], while some generalists are more likely to be able to do so[20]. Even exotic plants that are considered to be "naturalised" to their new environment support much lower numbers of insects in their new locations than in their original habitats. The process for them to become effectively integrated can take a long time, maybe even millenia.

Cycad Blue caterpillar on Japanese Sago Palm. This caterpillar also has a green colour form.   Dick Copeman

Research from a number of places around the world has shown that the number of different species (biodiversity) as well as the total numbers of insects (biomass or insect load) are both higher on native plants than on exotic plants. Conversely, if exotic plants displace native plants, both the biodiversity and biomass of insects is considerably reduced, with significant flow on effects on the ecosystem functions that insects perform.

*The rare case that almost proves the rule: the caterpillar of the Cycad Blue butterfly (**Theclinesthes onycha**), pictured here, is adapted to eating native cycad plants (**Macrozamia** spp). When a related plant, Japanese Sago palm (**Cycas revoluta**) was introduced as an ornamental plant, the species quickly adapted to this new host. The plant didn't have defence mechanisms or other features that make it hard to eat, and so the caterpillar and its butterfly flourished.*

In the US, studies by Tallamy found that native plants supported more than three times as many herbivore species and over four times as much herbivore biomass as exotic plants. When he looked just at the biomass of caterpillars of butterflies, moths and sawflies, the major food source for insectivorous birds, he found that native woody plants supported 35 times the biomass supported by exotic plants[12].

In both South Africa and the Azores, arthropod diversity at sites with few alien plants was higher than at sites with many alien plants[21, 22].

wingspan:
56mm

Yellow Migrant
Catopsilia gorgophone

other butterflies:
Large Grass-yellow

Climbing Senna
Senna gaudichaudii

Small
Grass-yellow

*Butterfly Lives: Lifecycle of, and host plant for, the Yellow Migrant, showing the adult butterfly with both open and closed wings, a mating pair, the caterpillar, chrysalises and a larval host plant. Also shown are two other species of butterflies, the Large Grass-yellow (**Eurema hecabe**) and the Small Grass-yellow (**Eurema smilax**) which can also use this host plant.*

www.earthling.com.au/butterfly-lives
Images by Helen Schwencke, except flower inset by Glenn Leiper, and Small Grass-yellow by Frank Jordan

A more recent review of 68 studies comparing herbivorous insects on native and non-native plants has shown that insect diversity was significantly higher on native than on non-native plants, while insect load tended to be higher on native plants but not to a statistically significant level[23].

Variability in outcomes between different studies is to be expected in a field where it is difficult to standardise methodology but the overwhelming evidence supports the idea that preserving the biodiversity of native insects requires the maintenance or restoration of healthy communities of the native host plants that support them.

Larval and adult food plants

Here is a key point that is little understood. Many herbivorous insects, such as butterflies and moths that have distinct larval and adult forms, require different food sources for the larval and adult forms. The food for the larvae, or caterpillars, is most often plant material such as leaves, flowers, seeds or fruit, while the food for the adult butterfly or moth is most often nectar from flowers. Another difference between the food sources for larval and adult forms is that larvae most often eat only one plant, or a small number of related plants, whereas the adults are often able to take nectar from many different flowers.

Many proponents of 'wildlife friendly gardening' focus on nectar plants for feeding birds, bees, and butterflies, with the bulk of those promoted being introduced ornamental plants or cultivars of native plants. These can appear to be very good at attracting insects because we can see lots of them coming and going around the plant. But when we look closely, we can notice, again with some exceptions, that there are no larval forms (caterpillars) on these good nectar plants. In general, they feed the adult butterflies and moths but not their larval forms.

*Climbing Senna (**Senna gaudichaudii**) (opposite) is an example of a plant that supports many insects. The leaves support the three butterflies shown, the flowers support the Pale Ciliated-blue (**Anthene lycaenoides**) and the flowers are pollinated by the buzz-pollinating bees, Teddy Bear bees, Large Carpenter bees, and Blue-banded bees (**Amegilla** spp.). The seed pods support the Large Brown Bean Bug (**Riptortus serripes**). On occasions various small birds, Grey Fantails and a female Robin, have been observed visiting the plant and catching butterflies.*

So the take home message here is that adult butterflies and moths will not come to your garden, in the numbers that help enhance biodiversity and can support your garden, if the food plant(s) for their caterpillars, often termed 'larval host plants' or just 'host plants', are not growing somewhere nearby.

Butterfly species vary greatly in their lifestyles. Some species stay within a short distance from their host plants but, more generally speaking, it is the role of the flying adult butterfly to venture into the big wide world and look for its food plants, especially if it has become crowded at home, and there are too many of their kind trying to use the same patch of host plants. A bit like when the wind blows seeds to new places, the butterfly is the dispersal mechanism for the species, so to speak, using nectar as its power supply. This is why you will have them visit your flowers, though they won't be able to create the next generation without the host plant(s) being present.

Some species disperse more spectacularly in some years, migrating seasonally in large masses over long distances, mostly over several generations, but that is a different story.

Pollination

Pollination of itself is a complex and fascinating subject. Here, we will be discussing pollination by insects. Pollination by wind is the other main type of pollination, though this is not part of our discussion here.

*Some plants, like the Climbing Senna above, need to be vibrated by native bees such as Blue-banded, Carpenter and Teddy Bear bees (**Amegilla** spp.) to release their pollen. Bees that buzz-pollinate can be heard making a distinctive sound when they do so - it can be a loud "buzz".*

As nectar feeding insects move from plant to plant, they pick up and carry pollen, some of which rubs off on other plants. If the pollen came from the same species of plant, it can then help pollinate the plants.

Our best known pollinators are bees but there are many other nectar eating insects that are also pollinators, including butterflies, moths, wasps, flies, beetles and ants. It is important to have a large variety of pollinators in your garden because flowers of different plants have various shapes and lengths, which are adapted to being pollinated by particular types of insect.

*A Blue-banded bee, male, (**Amegilla** spp.) that has pierced a flower at its base to access the nectar without there being any chance of pollination.*
Erica Siegel

There are some 1,500 named species of native bees in Australia, with estimates that there may be up to 2,000 species in total. Eleven species are social stingless bees. The remainder are either semi-social, for example, sharing an entrance to a burrow in the ground though which each female bee tends to her own offspring, or solitary. These bees have a wide variety of habitat and breeding requirements.

We have been led to believe that if you have a bee visiting your flowers, then you have a pollinator, but this is often not true. There are many examples where bees take nectar from flowers but do not perform pollination because they are too big, or are the wrong shape, for their pollen sacs to come into contact with the stigma of the flowers. In some cases, they even drill into the base of the flower to rob the nectar, avoiding the pollen on the anthers altogether, thereby robbing the pollinator species that is adapted to that flower of its meal, and the flower of the work it has done to produce the nectar.

Bees obtain all the food for both the adult (nectar) and the larva (pollen and nectar) from the flowers of the plants they visit but the larvae of the other pollinating insects listed above obtain their food from different sources to those that provide the adults with nectar, as discussed above. And some larvae, particularly those of wasps, are carnivores, eating other insects rather than plants.

So once again, the take home message is that if we want to attract the diverse range of insects that our plants need in order to be pollinated, then we need to ensure that the larval host plants and a variety of flowering plants are growing in our gardens or nearby. While this is important now, it will be even more important in the future if the numbers of that omni-present pollinator, the introduced European honey bee, are reduced by diseases or predators, as has happened in other countries.

Coming face-to-face with our subject

To help make our discussion come to life we need to learn to start noticing life in all its forms. Take a walk in your garden or some local bushland - look for locations that haven't been overwhelmed by introduced or invasive plants - or a nearby park or community garden, or any other setting where there are both plants and animals. It is also helpful to visit multiple sites on a number of occasions and compare your notes.

Share the experience with a friend or family members who are interested, if you can. Take your camera, preferably one with a macro lens or macro capability. Your phone's camera can often produce images that are good enough to help you identify what you are seeing.

Your task, should you choose to accept it, is to start exploring the amazing diversity of the little known life forms, and gain first hand experience of how they interact with each other.

Start learning to look for:

• **Chewed leaves on plants** - which creatures are doing the chewing and how many different species are there doing the chewing?

A Lemon Migrant caterpillar chewing the leaf of a host plant. Notice the smooth edge.
                                    Helen Schwencke

A Noctuid moth caterpillar chewing a native fig. Notice the jagged edge.   *Dick Copeman*

*Purple Moonbeam (**Philiris innotatus**) caterpillar skeletonising a Sandpaper Fig leaf (**Ficus opposita**), showing old (brownish) and new tracks (greenish).* Helen Schwencke

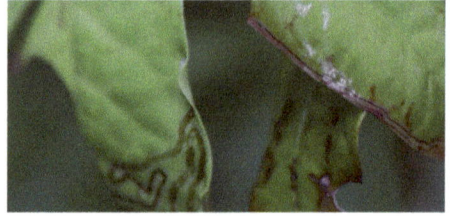

There are over 110 recorded species of leaf miners in Australia in four Orders: beetles, moths and butterflies, flies and wasps. Most are host-specific species of moth and fly larvae[24]. Helen Schwencke

*Galls are swellings induced by insect larvae of bugs, wasps, thrips, flies, beetles and moths as they feed on plant leaves and stems. Many feed on only one or a small number of plant species. This unidentified species is using Native Mulberry (**Pipturus argenteus**).* Helen Schwencke

*Red Triangle slugs (**Triboniophorus graeffei**) leave a rasping eating pattern on smooth tree trunks.* Helen Schwencke

*Large Brown Bean Bug (**Riptortus serripes**) is a native sap sucking bug (Order Hemiptera) that can also feed on introduced legume crops.* Dick Copeman

Bark Lice from the Order Psocodea, which includes some 11,000 species worldwide, including body lice. This species is piercing the stem and sucking sap. Helen Schwencke

- **Types of herbivory and plant use** - chewing, skeletonising, leaf mining, rasping, galling, piercing, sucking, rolling and shelter-building ... are illustrated here and there are so many more.

*A Bronze Flat caterpillar (****Netrocoryne repanda****) carefully and precisely cutting a leaf of a host plant to a specific shape to create the right pattern to fold and stitch into a shelter.*
Helen Schwencke

The shelter, which was built over two days, serves the caterpillar as a home and protection against predators for the remainder of its larval and pupal stages.
Helen Schwencke

*Many species of moth and a few butterflies have shelter-building caterpillars. This is an unidentified species that stitched a whole compound **Flindersia** sp. leaf together. Caterpillar inset.*
Ute Harder de Sohnrey

*Leafcutter Bees (**Megachile** spp.) build shelters from overlapping scales of soft, broad-leaved plants to create cells that they provision with pollen and nectar for the next generation. Round cuts are used for the caps of each cell, while rounded-oblong shapes are cut for the scales. Both types of scales are shown having been cut from Native Plumbago (**Plumbago zeylanica**) leaves. Females use a variety of locations, such as holes in wood or earth or folds in cloth, to house their leaf-scale cells. These cells were built in a folded old sock left on a protected washing line. The holes in the two separated cells on the LHS show that the bees had emerged. The female bee shown here is starting to cut a Native Mulberry leaf and is possibly **M. ignescens**, one of at least 35 Australian species, as last described in 1965.*
Helen Schwencke

- **Characteristics of the host plants** (the plants being chewed):
  - Tree, shrub, vine, ground cover, grass, etc.
  - Leaves, flowers and fruit - their shape, size and colour
  - Roots

Look at the texture of the leaves, bark, stems, or other plant part you can see being used. Is it smooth, hairy, thick or thin, waxy or not, tough or soft, young or old growth? Can you see any ways that the plant is using to defend itself mechanically?

*Stinging Nettle (**Urtica incisa**) has a formidable defence mechanism to prevent being eaten - needle sharp shards that sting painfully. Yellow Admiral caterpillars (**Vanessa itea**) have found a way to manage this defence and happily eat the leaves and turn them into a shelter.*   Helen Schwencke

*Wilkiea macrophylla, a rainforest understorey plant, retains its leaves for the longest time known for any Australian plant - six to twelve years. Their new growth thickens and hardens rapidly, which makes them unpalatable to many herbivores. However, Regent Skipper butterfly caterpillars (**Euschemon rafflesia**) get round this defence by scraping the underside of the leaves.*   Helen Schwencke

- **Delightful surprises**

*Caper White (**Belenois java**) eggs hatching.*   Annette Dexter

*A Wattle Prominent Moth caterpillar, **Neola semiaurata**, frightening off humans and predators alike with the large eyespot at its tail end.*   Helen Schwencke

*A male bottle cicada, probably a **Chlorocysta** sp. that has successfully advertised his real estate and won a mate by making a piercingly loud, shrill call from a Black thorn (**Bursaria spinosa**) tree.*   Helen Schwencke

- **Mimicry**

*Early stage nymphs of the Large Brown Bean Bug (**Riptortus serripes**) (see page 26) mimic ants, as do many other creatures.*   Helen Schwencke

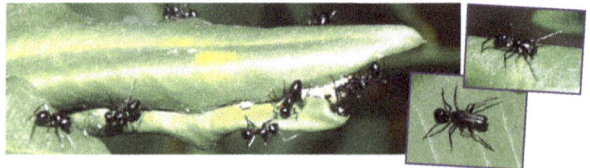

*Rattle ants, **Polyrachis** sp. build their colonies by stitching leaves together. They are adapting to gardens and will take up residence in any narrow tubes or pipes that we leave lying around. When disturbed, they defend their nest by coming out and tapping their abdomens against the leaves. An ant-mimicking spider, **Myrmarachne** sp., may be observed near their nests. The juvenile and female spiders (top RHS) resemble the ants quite closely while adult males (bottom RHS) develop a more spider-like appearance.*   Helen Schwencke

- **Scavenging and decomposing**

*An unidentified species of ant, possibly an introduced Tramp ant, **Technomyrmex albipes**, eating a dead caterpillar.*
Ants play diverse ecological roles as scavengers, decomposers, predators, farmers, seed harvesters and dispersers, soil aerators, pollinators and even as protectors of some caterpillars. There are up to 350 species of ants in the Brisbane region alone[40].
Annette Dexter

*An obscured entrance to a burrow of a giant earthworm native to south-east QLD, possibly a **Digaster** sp. Earthworms play a vital role in nutrient cycling, creating fertile soils and maintaining plant health. Australia has a diverse earthworm fauna with around 650 described native species in 45 genera, many of which are endemic to specific areas. There are also 65 introduced species that are more generalist and more that are as yet undescribed. Each species has its own role and position, e.g. some are deep burrowers and others shallow burrowers[41].*
Helen Schwencke

Learning to observe the small creatures around you and the plants they inhabit can turn any walk anywhere into an exciting exploration as you start noticing and identifying life in all its forms.

As you engage with the natural world, it helps to be aware of your "point of view" in a literal, as well as figurative sense. We see things most frequently when they are in our eye scanning range, which is at eye level and a bit below and above. We may see a myriad of insects feeding on the flowers of a particular plant growing at our eye level and assume that that plant is an important one for those insects. But we may miss seeing all the other insects feeding on different plants higher in the canopy, unless we use a good set of binoculars.

This selective perception can bias our understanding and influence which plants we choose to enhance our biodiversity. So we need to observe life in all layers of the bush, from soil to canopy, and to select plants for all those layers for our gardens.

The ultimate way to identify a larval form (caterpillar or grub) is to raise it yourself, feeding it on leaves from the plant on which you found it. That way you can observe and photograph its whole life cycle up to the adult stage, which makes it easier to identify, usually! There is still much that is not known about the life cycles of many creatures, and which larvae or nymphs belong to which adults.

Resources

Books, websites, social media pages and institutions that can help you identify plants and creatures are listed at the end of this book, as are relevant clubs and organisations with like-minded members who are usually only too willing to welcome you and help guide your learning journey. See list of websites, p. 104.

4. Wildlife-friendly gardening

How to support native wildlife in your garden

Grow local native plants

- *Select plants that are native to your local bio-region, or ideally your catchment.*

Old Man Banksia **(Banksia integrifolia)**   Dick Copeman

These plants of 'local provenance' will support more local native wildlife than plants that are native to other bioregions of Australia. They are best sourced from local nurseries or plant societies (see Appendix 3 and list of websites on p. 104) for a list of nurseries and plant societies that supply local native plants for the Macleay McPherson Overlap bioregion in SE QLD and N NSW.)

- *Select plants from the broad vegetation group that grew before European settlement in the place where your property is located.*

The key distinction here is between closed forest or rainforest, and open forest or sclerophyll forest. Rainforest plants in general have larger, shinier leaves and shallower root systems, they require more regular water and the smaller plants are more shade tolerant. Plants from open, sclerophyll forests tend to have narrower, duller leaves that often hang downwards, their roots are deeper and they are more drought resistant but less shade tolerant.

Maps of broad vegetation types are available on-line via the link in Appendix 1: Site Assessment and Analysis. Nurseries and plant identification reference books such as Mangroves to Mountains (see reference in Bibliography) can help you select the right types of plants for your location.

- *Avoid plants that are commercial hybrids or cultivars.*

These have been cross-bred or selected for particular traits, such as colour of flowers or leaves, duration of flowering or dwarf form. Anecdotal evidence from gardeners is that these usually attract less diversity of local native wildlife, though there is no research evidence on this, one way or the other. It may be that the local insects are not able to cope with the phytochemicals in the hybrids, as discussed in the Plants and Insects section above regarding plant defence chemicals. These commercial hybrids and cultivars are also mostly developed for the larger markets of southern Australian cities, using species from those regions, so they may not grow as well as plants from your local area.

Grow a diverse range of plants

- **Select plants with varied growth habits and forms.**

Plants vary in habit and form from tall to medium to small trees, shrubs, vines, scramblers, grasses, herbs, forbs and groundcovers, and they arrange themselves naturally in a series of layers. The more you can mimic that pattern in your garden, the more habitat for small creatures there will be and the more attractive your garden will look. Some of these forms can be placed in an organised way, while some, especially the vines and the ground covers, are best left to grow where they choose.

- **Include fast and slow growing plants and be prepared to manage their growth and succession.**

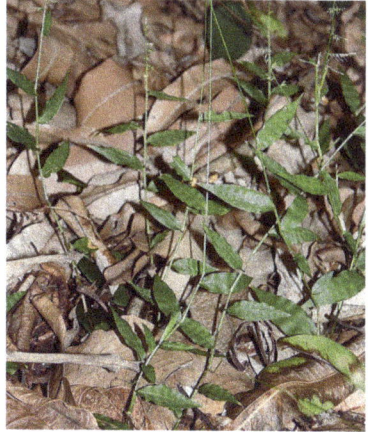

*Ground cover: Creeping Beard Grass (**Oplismenus aemulus**). Helen Schwencke*

Pioneer plants grow quickly, filling gaps, but then die back as slower growing species emerge and form a canopy. Open areas are best for sun-loving plants which will die back once a canopy forms and they are in the shade, and will then need to be replaced by shade tolerant species. Accept that disturbance, such as limbs dropping due to storms, wind, disease or insect damage, can create sunny spots that can be filled with new species. You can even create your own disturbance by some strategic pruning.

- **Avoid monocultures and don't plant too many of the one species.**

*Kangaroo grass (**Themeda triandra**). Dick Copeman*

As gardeners, we all have our favourite plants but we need to resist the temptation to plant too many of them all together. If we create a virtual monoculture, we simplify our garden ecosystem and reduce the biodiversity of its plants and invertebrate wildlife.

Plants such as Mat Rush (*Lomandra* spp.), Lilly pillies (*Syzygium* spp.) and *Westringia* spp. are all excellent native habitat and nectar plants but they are often used too frequently in gardens and public spaces. Take a walk through some native bush near your property to observe the diversity of species and use that as the model for planting in your garden.

*Small-leaved Lilli pilli (**Syzygium leuh-mannii**)*   *Dick Copeman*

There are over 360 known and verified native plant species in the SEQ and N NSW that support the 200 butterflies which occur in this region. Comprehensive lists for moth and other insect larval host plants are yet to be developed.

*Love Flower (**Pseuderanthemum variabile**), host plant for five butterflies. It is a highly variable plant.*   *Helen Schwencke*

Small-leaved Lilly pillies (*Syzygium leuhmannii*) is an attractive medium sized bushtucker tree and its flowers provide nectar but it has been overplanted in previous years. Its roots can be very competitive and can also block drains.

Grow host plants for caterpillars other insect larvae

- **To support butterfly caterpillars, plant their host plants, including:**

Caper bushes, native mulberry, senna and cassia shrubs, native grasses, sedges, mat rushes, wattles, native passion vines, and the many other plants listed in Appendix 2 and in Butterfly Host Plants of SE QLD and N NSW.

As you watch these host plants grow, you will find that your inherent bias in favour of neat, whole leaves on your plants will reverse and you will start to rejoice when you see leaves with holes or chew marks. You will be eagerly turning them over to see if you can spot the caterpillars that are eating them and when you do, you will be proudly showing them to your family and friends.

- **To support moth caterpillars, plant:**

Native grapes, banksias, gum trees, native mulberry, acronychias, macadamias and many, many others.

The vast majority of moths are active only at night, and their larvae are often harder to find

It is estimated there are between 20,000 and 40,000 species of butterflies and moths in Australia (Order Lepidoptera). 405 of these are named butterflies, in five butterfly Families. The remainder are moths in 69 families, many of which are still to be named, and their lifecycles are yet to be understood.

during the day, so their life cycles and host plants have not been as well documented as those of butterflies. However, there are some quite large and spectacular moth caterpillars that are readily visible in the daytime, as shown here.

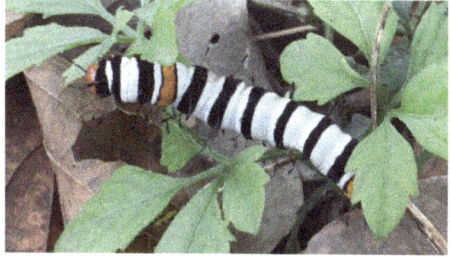

*Caterpillar of Joseph's Coat moth (**Agarista agricola**) on Slender Grape (**Cayratia clematidea**).*
Dick Copeman

Grow local native flowering plants, especially those that are good nectar producers

Flowers add beauty and colour to any garden and their nectar is an important food for the adult forms of many insects, such as butterflies, moths, bees, wasps, beetles and flies, as well as for birds.

- **Smaller native plants that are good nectar producers include:**

  Native daisies and other plants in the Asteraceae family, Fan flowers, Bursarias, Banksias, Grevilleas, Hakeas, Parsonsia vines, Pigface and Legumes including Hardenbergia, Daviesia, Hovea, Jacksonia, Gompholobium, and Dillwynia.

- **Larger native plants that are good nectar and pollen producers include:**

  Myrtles, Lilly pillies, Gum trees and Tea trees.

The invasive roots and large size of these members of the Myrtaceae family can cause problems for other nearby plants and therefore require careful design and placement if they are included in a garden. Smaller members of this family, such as some of the leptospermums and sannanthas, are more suited as nectar plants for a smaller home garden.

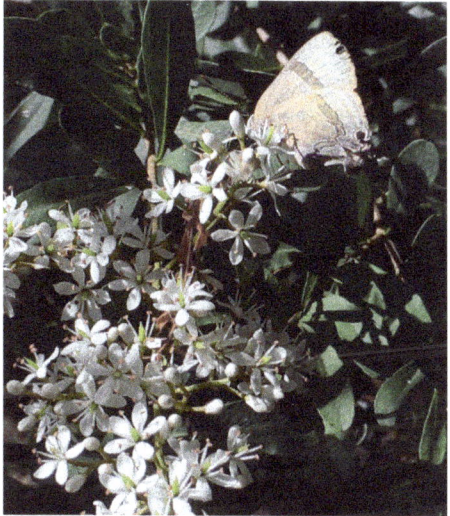

*Indigo Flash (**Rapala varuna**) feeding on the flowers of Black Thorn (**Bursaria spinosa**).*
Dick Copeman

*A Fiddler beetle (**Eupoecila australasiae**) and Stingless Bees (**Tetragonula** sp.) feeding on the flowers of the Pink Bloodwood (**Corymbia intermedia**).*   *Dick Copeman*

- *Select a range of flowering plants that together produce flowers throughout the year*

Most plants flower from late winter through spring and into early summer but native daisies, fan flowers, Westringias, Grevilleas, Parsonsias and Bursarias have extended flowering periods.

Grow local native plants that are edible

- *Many native plants produce nuts, seeds, fruit, leaves, flowers or roots that are edible by humans.*

Zig Zag Vine (**Melodorum leichhardtii**) has tangy fruit and is host for three butterflies.   Dick Copeman

Millaa Millaa Vine (**Eleagnus triflora**), with its tasty fruit, is host for the Indigo Flash (**Rapala varuna**) butterfly.
          Dick Copeman

First Nations Australians have harvested, cultivated and eaten these plants for thousands of years and, in recent years, settler Australians have come to realise their potential as 'new' foods and flavours. Many of these bushfoods are also food for insects and other invertebrates, as listed in Appendix 2: Some plants (mostly Edible) that pupport butterflies and other wildlife in south east Queensland and northern NSW.

By growing, preparing and eating these bushfoods, we are not only acknowledging the heritage we have gained from the first Australians but we are also, in a sense, 'sharing' these foods with our more distant invertebrate relatives. Section 8 includes recipes for preparing and cooking some of these shared bushfoods.

Attract native wildlife to your vegetable garden and orchard

- *Replace exotic support plants with local native plant species where possible*

Many exotic herbs and ornamental plants, including some that are promoted as "Good Bug Mix", produce flowers that attract and feed insects, but these are mainly introduced honey bees, and they support little biodiversity compared to local native plants.

Instead of these exotic plants, try native daisies, fan flowers, native violets and Emu foot (*Cullen tenax*) between and around your vegetables, and native Plumbago

(*Plumbago zeylanica*) and Coastal Boobialla (*Myoporum boninense* var. *australe*) as ground covers in your orchard. Native legumes such as Sennas, Indigoferas, and the smaller Acacias grown between and around your fruit trees will not only attract insects and other invertebrates, but will also add nitrogen to the soil.

- *Let vegetables and herbs go to flower and seed*

The flowers will provide pollen and nectar for native bees and other pollinator insects while letting them set seed will provide food for birds. Flowering herbs such as rosemary and lavender will attract generalist native bees such as the Blue-banded Bee and lettuce that is left to go to seed has been known to be eaten by Pale-headed Rosellas.

- *Leave a few weeds to set flowers*

Until you have a range of native nectar and pollen producing plants that flower across the seasons, the flowers of Cobblers' Pegs (*Bidens pilosa*) are a good nectar source for insects, but make sure you slash or dig them in before they set seed. Other weeds that produce copious nectar that attracts insects include spurge (*Euphorbia* spp.) and Lantana but keeping these plants in your garden is not recommended in the long term.

- *Leave some bare soil in your garden*

This allows ground-dwelling native bees to build their burrows.

- *Recognise that a few exotic food plants can be host plants for native butterflies.*

Exotic citrus and custard apple trees, for example, are hosts to the caterpillars of the Orchard Swallowtail and Pale Triangle butterflies respectively. With established plants, they rarely eat enough to make a noticeable difference.

Grow plants with dense or prickly foliage

- *Include some tall grasses and dense shrubs*

Kangaroo grass (*Themeda triandra*), Tussock grass (*Poa labillardieri*), Saw sedges (*Gahnia* spp), Mat rushes (*Lomandra* spp), Glossy Cough bush (*Cassinia subtropica*), Hop bushes (*Dodonaea* spp), Poison peach (*Trema tomentosa*) and Finger lime (*Citrus australasica*) are just some of the plants that can provide habitat where insects such as praying mantids and assassin bugs can hunt their prey.

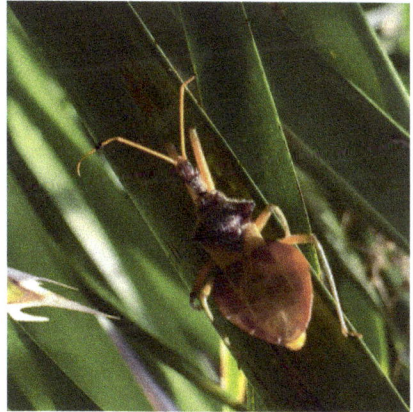

Assassin bug, Family Reduviidae, hiding in Mat Rush (**Lomandra** sp.)   Dick Copeman

- *Plant mixed species hedges of prickly plants*

Finger Lime (**Citrus australasica**), grafted
specimen   Dick Copeman

Finger lime (*Citrus australasica*), currant bush (*Carissa ovata*), black thorn (*Bursaria spinosa*), cockspur (*Maclura cochinchinensis*) and chain fruit (*Alyxia ruscifolia*) provide safe habitat for small birds that help moderate population explosions of competitor insects.

In south-east Queensland small birds are known to over-winter in mixed species flocks in dense vegetation. For example, in winter 2011 at Federation Lookout, Mt Gravatt, over the span of 15 minutes, Helen observed 12 different bird species flying in and out of the dense vegetation. Let's look for ways to recreate this habitat in the suburbs.

Grow plants that produce a lot of seed or fruit

- *Seed producing native plants include:*

Many grasses as well as hakeas, acacias and pigface. They produce many seeds that are food for birds, especially the smaller birds that help keep populations of competitor insects in check.

- *Fruit producing native plants include:*

Sandpaper fig (**Ficus coronata**) has sweet
and juicy fruit, is host for two butterflies
and attracts many birds, beetles and other
insects.   Glenn Leiper

Trees such as tuckeroos (*Cupaniopsis* spp), figs (*Ficus* spp), Lilly pillies, (*Syzygium* spp),

*Many gardens contain introduced plants that produce fruit and seeds. Some birds have adapted to these species and are now spreading them throughout urban areas and into local bushland. **Duranta**, **Murraya** spp, **Ochna** and Chinese elms (**Celtis** sp.) are just a few of the more common ones. As stands of these species develop, they displace native plant species, ecologically simplifying bushland areas and reducing food sources for native animals. We need to give birds native plant fruit and seeds to disperse so they can do some of the revegetation work that is needed and we can effortlessly enjoy the process.*

Alectryon spp and *Elaeocarpus* spp., shrubs such as caper bushes, coffee bush and lime berries, vines such as native grapes (*Cissus* spp., *Cayratia clematidea*) and shrubs such as Native Mulberry (*Pipturus argenteus*). They provide food for insects as well as larger birds, mammals and reptiles. See also Appendix 2 for many more suggestions.

Leave the old and the dead in place

- ### Large old trees develop tree hollows

These take many decades to form and provide nesting and living spaces for spiders, native bees, beetles, birds, insectivorous bats, reptiles, possums and gliders. If dead trees are removed and replaced by new plantings, it takes many years for them to develop new hollows.

- ### Dead branches provide roosting and nesting spots for birds and gliders as well as sites for spiders' webs.

- ### Leaf litter and fallen bark should, where possible, be left on the ground.

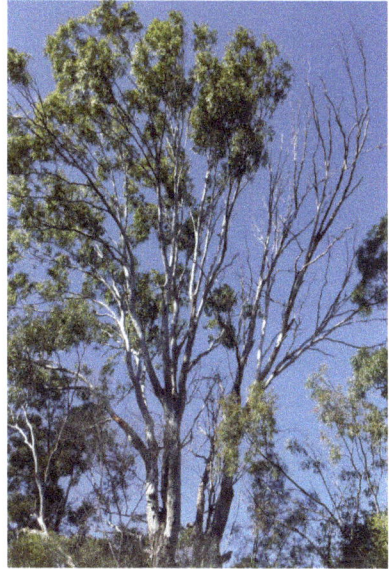

As long as there is no safety risk, dead limbs are best left on trees.   Dick Copeman

It is important food for some moth larvae, native cockroaches, earthworms, and many other invertebrates, including mites and springtails.

Termites have an important role in developing tree hollows.
There are around 360 species of termites in Australia, and only nine have the potential to cause any problems to our structures built of wood, and several of these have been introduced to Australia.
Native termites play an essential ecological role in decomposing wood and grasses and recycling nutrients especially in the more arid areas of Australia. Various Kingfishers, including Kookaburras, rely on arboreal nesting termites for their places to breed.

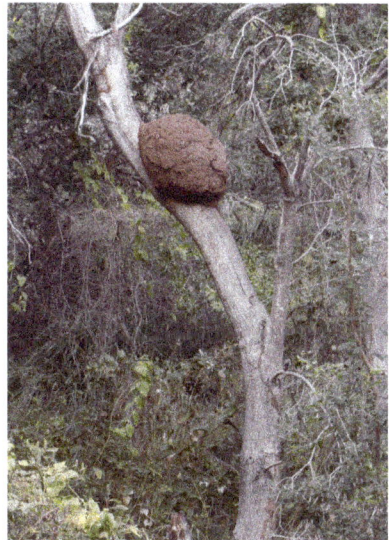

A termite nest in a tree. You can safely leave these where they are. Arboreal (tree based) species do not cause any damage to our houses.   Helen Schwencke

- *Fallen logs are also best left on the ground.*

Fallen log with nest holes, an ant and an all but invisible spider.   *Dick Copeman*

They are eaten by termites and the larvae of many families of beetles and of some moths and flies. The droppings of all these animals replenish the soil by recycling nutrients back into it. Holes in dead timber provide nesting sites for solitary bees such as carpenter, resin and leaf-cutter bees.

Did you know there are over 530 species of native cockroaches in Australia? Ten species have been introduced and they make up the majority of those that come into houses. There are a number of flightless species where females give birth to live babies and they show maternal care and live in family groups. Many native cockroaches play essential decomposer roles in ecosystems.

*A diurnal (day-active) nymph stage of a bush roach (**Ellipsidion** sp.) that has a varied diet, including moulds on dead leaves.*   *Helen Schwencke*

Protect and nurture the soil

- *Avoid clearing, ploughing or over-digging*

  These disturbances can rapidly erode and degrade your soil as minerals are leached out by heavy rain and organic matter is oxidised by sunlight. They also disrupt the life cycles of the many insects and other invertebrates that live part of their lives in the soil.

- *Minimize disturbance of soil and soil seed banks*

  When weeding, especially in areas where native ground covers have been incorporated into your planting, consider cutting off the unwanted plants at the roots using a sharp serrated steak knife to achieve as little disturbance as possible.

- *Plant a combination of ground cover plants and taller plants*

  These ensure that there are plenty of roots and leaves to hold and protect the soil and to nourish the larvae and other life-forms that feed on roots and soil micro-organisms.

- ***Leave a layer of dead leaves and other organic debris on top of the soil***

This protects the soil and provides food for the many insects and other invertebrates that eat and recycle this organic material. It is best, however, to avoid over-application of fibrous mulch, as it can inhibit natural regeneration of native plants, facilitate invasive weeds and change the composition of the soil micro-fauna.

- ***Include legumes in your plant mix***

These help replenish the nitrogen in the soil by 'fixing' nitrogen from the atmosphere into the soil with the help of bacterial nodules on their roots.

Provide water

- ***Capture the rain that falls on your garden***

Maintain good levels of spongy humus in your soil to ensure that the water soaks in and is retained in the soil. On slopes, you can also use swales, shallow ditches that run along the contours, to intercept water run off and help it infiltrate into the soil. Tanks can capture water that falls on the roofs of houses and sheds, and that water can then be used in dry periods for additional watering by hand or by drip irrigation.

- ***Install a pond or a bog garden***

Insects, particularly dragonflies and damselflies, as well as frogs, reptiles and birds, require regular access to open water, while many other insects just need moist soil in a boggy area or soak. Create these spaces so they mimic natural areas these species would use, where they are in contact with the soil and are protected to prevent predators. Avoid bird baths, especially if they aren't cleaned regularly, as they can facilitate the spread of wildlife diseases.

Some butterfly host plants that grow well in a bog garden or soak include:

*Arrowhead Violet (**Viola betonicifolia**)*
Dick Copeman

- Karamat (*Hygrophila angustifolia*) which supports up to five different butterflies.

- Arrowhead Violet (*Viola betonicifolia*) supports the Laced Fritillary, which is endangered, and may already be extinct.

- Saltbush (*Atriplex* spp.), Berry Saltbush (*Einadia hastata*) and other *Einadia* spp. support the Saltbush blue butterfly.

- Mangrove Wax-flower (*Cynanchum carnosum*) is a mainly ground covering vine that grows near mangrove edges and supports three butterflies.

Don't use pesticides and other toxic chemicals in your garden

With insects comprising the largest amount of animal biodiversity on our little blue planet, if we try to control them using poisonous chemicals, we have to recognise that they have the numbers and will always win in the end. We will never succeed. Such an approach is not only a lost cause but also causes serious collateral damage to other species and the environment. We need to work with insects rather than against them.

Look back at the "Insects relative to all other animals" diagram on page 11, which shows the little dot in the middle that represents those insect species that have the potential to have a serious effect on our crops. Comparing its size to that of the large circle, which represents the vast bulk of all other animals, shows that we need to consider how our use of pesticides to attempt to control that small group can have serious effects on the large numbers of other creatures.

So, if you are faced with an explosion of insects that are eating your food plants, don't reach for the spray bottle. Instead, try to work out why they are there in such numbers. It could be that you have planted too many of the same plant together, creating a 'monoculture' that has become a magnet for the plant eating insects. Or maybe you don't have many spiders or predatory insects in your garden because you don't have any dead logs, shrubby vegetation or flowering native plants to provide their habitat and food. Go through the list of actions above and check that your garden is providing the habitat and environment to support 'ally' animals such as spiders, small wasps, hoverflies, bees, birds, reptiles and frogs that will help keep competitor insect populations in check.

In the meantime, while you get your wildlife friendly garden sorted, instead of toxic chemicals, you could use:

- **Physical control methods**
  - Remove caterpillars and grasshoppers by hand when they are sluggish in the early morning
  - Put fine netting over your brassicas to keep cabbage white butterflies from laying their eggs on your plants
  - Hose aphids off growing tips

*The natural spray, Bt (**Bacillus thuringiensis**), a soil bacterium, is allowed to be used by organic farmers to control caterpillars because it is safe for humans. However, it will kill all caterpillars, not just those that are causing the problem, so is best avoided in your garden.*

- **Home remedy sprays**
  - Spray with diluted soap and oil spray to reduce damage from sap-sucking insects without affecting your garden environment.

You can also help reduce the amount of pesticides applied to food crops by farmers if you buy certified organic food, which is produced without using pesticides, when you purchase food for yourself and your family.

How to plan a wildlife friendly garden

Planning a garden is an exercise in match-making - matching the plants to the garden site. Each garden site has its unique features of soil, climate, vegetation and water. Each plant also has its own unique characteristics such as size, growth habit and flowering season, as well as specific conditions it needs for optimal growth and productivity, including the climate and soil it has evolved in and its requirements for water, drainage, sunlight, pollination, etc.

Many plants fail to thrive because all these features are not fully considered. A plant from a different climate or requiring a different soil type, or one that is too large for the site or surrounded by inappropriate companions, will struggle to survive, let alone thrive, no matter how much water, fertiliser or mulch is applied to it.

We should also plan our gardens to nourish and enhance the environment by including plants that provide food and shelter for animals, large and small, and by selecting and placing our plants so that they can perform "ecosystem functions" including protecting and replenishing the soil, allowing water to seep into the soil, stabilising slopes, cleaning the air, and sheltering other plants from excessive wind or sun.

Goals for the garden

We can have many different goals for our gardens. Some of us may wish to produce food and other useful products such as medicinal herbs, fabric dyes, weaving material or firewood, while others prefer to grow flowers and other ornamental plants. Most of us also want our garden to be visually attractive and to provide a restful retreat that is also a social space to share with our family and friends.

No matter what the focus of your garden is, it is always possible to include plants that provide habitat and food for local native wildlife, not only for the more obvious birds and lizards but also for the less obvious but just as important smaller creatures such as insects, worms and frogs.

Other considerations

Ensuring that our gardens enhance the environment, and do not degrade it, requires that we use water and energy efficiently and that we are careful and sparing in our use of external resources.

Before starting to create a new garden or retrofitting an existing one, it also helps to have a clear idea of how much you are willing to spend on it and how much time and energy you will have for installing and maintaining it.

Sketch a plan

Sketching out your ideas can help with the planning of a garden. For this, you will need a base plan of the garden site, with its boundaries and existing features marked on it. Base plans can be adapted from on-line or local government maps, or drawn from scratch from measurements on the ground.

Assess and analyse your site

To understand what your site has to offer and what its limitations may be, you will need to identify and record the following information:

This section provides a general outline of how to do a site assessment. Detailed training in how to draw up a base plan and how to assess and analyse a site is provided by Permaculture Design Certificate Courses that are run in many locations throughout Australia and overseas. Go to https:// permacultureaustralia.org.au/events/ list/ for a list of just some of the courses on offer.

- The geology of the underlying terrain and the shape and slope of the site.

- The type of soil, its pH, drainage rate, and any toxins it may contain.

- The original native vegetation on the site, the plants that are there now and any wildlife and competitor species.

- The seasonal patterns of rainfall, temperature and wind, the likelihood of drought, flood, cyclone and fire, and predictions for future changes in the climate.

- The microclimate of the various different parts of your garden - seasonal patterns of sun and shade, wind, soil moisture and frost.

- Sources of water, how it flows across your site, and any boggy areas or dry spots.

- Buildings and other structures on or adjoining the site, the location of utility lines, activity nodes and the flows of people, vehicles and materials across the site.

- The aesthetics of the site, including views, sight lines, unattractive areas and noise.

- Legal issues, including zoning, covenants, setbacks, easements, body corporate rules, local plant and weed regulations, etc.

Record these 'layers' of site characteristics as one or more annotated sketches on the base plan. Appendix 1: Site assessment and analysis gives a detailed outline for SE Queensland of how to obtain details of this information, including relevant websites. Similar information sources are available for other regions of Australia.

Select your plants

Obtain information about plants that are adapted to the conditions of your garden by first finding out the original native vegetation of your site from the links listed in Appendix 1. Observing the local native plants that grow well in local reserves, parks and gardens in your neighbourhood can also give you inspiration.

A list of plants native to the SEQ region which support insects and smaller animals, and many of which produce food, is included in Appendix 2: Some plants (mostly edible) that support butterflies and other wildlife in south east Queensland and northern NSW. They are grouped according to plant size and form, with some information on sun and water requirements and other particular characteristics, needs and functions.

Information about non-native or 'exotic' vegetable and fruit plants can be obtained from local nurseries and from gardening books written by local hort-iculturalists. Many of the vegetables and fruits sold in fruit shops and supermarkets have been brought in from other climatic regions and are not easily grown locally. However, there are many others that originate from regions in other countries with similar climates that are more easily grown. Information about these is available from permaculture sources and nurseries.

Obtain your desired plants from wherever you can - friends, permaculture and gardening groups, local nurseries, your local council, etc. See Appendix 3 for a list of nurseries in SE QLD and N NSW.

From these various sources of information, select plants that are adapted to the conditions of your garden and that also serve your goals for your garden - food, flowers, shade, supporting wildlife etc. - while keeping within your budget and resource constraints.

Place your plants

Using multiple copies of the base plan, start sketching possible locations for the selected plants, taking into account their characteristics, needs and functions and their relationships with each other. This sketching is best done out in the garden, where the plants can be visualised, rather than sitting at a desk. Start with a sketch of the larger plants at the size they will be when they are mature to ensure that there will be sufficient room for them all. Check their placement against the site analysis sketch to ensure that each plant is positioned so that it receives the appropriate amount of sun, shade, water and wind at the various seasons of the year and that it can be accessed as required for care and harvesting. Check also that it is in the right position to be able to serve the various functions that you would like it to perform e.g. as a windbreak, to provide shade or to frame a good view.

Once you have decided where to put the larger plants, sketch them again on a new sheet in the same location but this time sketch them at their sizes when first planted. Then select smaller plants and plants with shorter lifespans to fill in the gaps between the larger plants while they are getting established and growing to their mature size.

Select plants that serve a range of functions, including:

- Legumes that replenish soil nitrogen

- Fast growing plants that can be 'chopped and dropped' to provide mulch and soil carbon

- Host plants that provide food and habitat for insect larvae.

- Flowering plants that provide nectar and pollen for adult insects. Aim to include plants that flower at different times of the year so as to provide a continuous source of nectar and pollen for the insects.

- Plants that provide habitat and shelter for animals, such as prickly bushes, clumping grasses, trees with rough bark, old trees with hollows, etc.

- Your initial selection of these 'infill' or support plants should be plants that tolerate sun, but as the larger plants grow and a canopy forms, they may need to be replaced with plants that tolerate shade, while still serving the functions listed above.

Instead of, or in addition to, selecting and placing these infill plants, you can do what Helen does and simply obtain seed of suitable native plants and plant or broadcast it without any follow up care. This is essentially a form of trial and error, in which any seeds that do manage to germinate, grow and survive will be adapted to local conditions of climate, soil and wildlife.

An example of a developed wildlife-friendly garden

Photos of Helen's West End house and garden, front (with obscuring thumb) on the left, back on the right, at time of purchase in 1987. There was a grass patch at the front and a vegetable garden along with a few Mediterranean fruit trees in the back garden.   *Helen Schwencke*

Photos, taken in 2018 from similar positions, are of the same house and transformed garden, front and back. This 33 year old butterfly and wildlife garden was developed through a mixture of planned and trial and error strategies. It comprises a mix of subtropical exotic fruit trees, butterfly and wildlife supporting plants including local native bush food.   *Helen Schwencke*

Native food plants we can share

The first Australians have lived here for 65,000 years, surviving on native plants and animals. The Europeans who forcibly settled the country over the past 230 years mostly ignored these native foods, cultivating instead the plants and animals they were familiar with from their home countries.

When home gardeners realised in the 1970s that native plants were often easier to grow as ornamental plants than exotic plants and could be just as attractive, if not more so, some went further and investigated whether some of them could also be eaten by humans. Guided by the knowledge of surviving indigenous people and by records from early settlers, and confirmed in some cases by laboratory analysis, scientists and others published books on so-called 'bush foods' or 'bush tucker', native plants that produce fruit, seeds, leaves or shoots that can safely be eaten by humans.

Bush food gardens were planted by enthusiasts in parks, community gardens and backyards. A small bush food industry developed also, growing mainly native spices, nuts and fruits for gourmet restaurants. More recently, younger and urban indigenous people have begun to reclaim the heritage of edible plants that their ancestors harvested and sometimes cultivated.

In tandem with the growing interest in native plants, more scientists and amateur naturalists have become interested in Australia's spectacular range of butterflies, in particular, and invertebrates in general. As we have become aware of the relationships between these small creatures and the plants on which they depend for their food and shelter, we have realised that many of these plants are edible or bushfood plants.

Thus arose the notion that we as humans can plant and nurture bushfood plants with the aim of 'sharing' them with our fellow creatures, particularly the small invertebrates. We can both obtain food from them and we can help ensure their survival and the maintenance of a healthy ecology in our gardens and local communities.

For a list of some plants (mostly edible) that support butterflies and other wildlife in south east Queensland, please see Appendix 2. The plants are grouped according to their size and form and there is information about their characteristics, needs and functions, their edible parts and the butterflies and other wildlife they support. The major support they provide is as host plants for the larvae (caterpillars) of butterflies and moths. The flowers of most of these plants also provide food for the adult butterflies and moths in the form of nectar, but some of the plants listed are specifically identified as particularly good sources of nectar, not only for butterflies but also for other insects including bees, wasps and hoverflies, as well as for birds.

The remainder of this chapter contains illustrated case studies of native food plants that are also food for butterfly larvae. Helen has personally grown all these plants and observed the butterfly larvae and adults on them in her garden in inner Brisbane or at Woodfordia, so they provide a proven group of plants for gardeners to try in their own gardens.

Butterflies feature predominantly in these case studies and also in Appendix 2, not only because their caterpillars are a highly visible group of invertebrate herbivores but also because they have been more thoroughly studied. Their ecological relationships are well understood and their host plants are known.

There is less knowledge about other groups of invertebrates but it is known that the larvae of many moths, of which there are many more than of butterflies, are also dependent on specific host plants, and some of these are listed in Appendix 2.

Where images are available for other creatures, that are supported by the host plants discussed here, they will be added to the next edition.

Case studies of native food plants that are also food for butterfly larvae and other wildlife

The insect food plants, described in detail in the following pages, grow at a variety of different levels in the canopy, and in a variety of habitats and are a small sample of plants that can be grown in a smaller garden. Many of these have been trialled on Helen's property, a 405sq m block in inner Brisbane, or at Woodfordia, site of the Woodford Folk Festival, in the butterfly and other invertebrates biodiversity plantings.

While the plants discussed here are primarily larval food plants, many will also provide nectar to feed the adult butterflies.

The images included in this section are from Helen's extensive collection of butterfly lifecycle and ecology interpretation signs, called Butterfly Lives. Each panel shows at least one aspect of the adult butterfly, a caterpillar and a chrysalis along with a host plant for that species of butterfly.

Jezebel Nymph
Mynes geoffroyi

wingspan:
50 - 57mm

♂

♀

other butterflies:
Speckled Line-blue

Native Mulberry
Pipturus argenteus ♀

© photos by Helen Schwencke, 2016   **www.earthling.com.au**   © Earthling Enterprises, 2016

Native Mulberry, female plant, showing the small white fruit, with two species of butterflies that use it as a host plant. The top half shows the Jezebel Nymph, with the open-winged adults at the top left and the more frequently seen closed-wing butterfly on the right. Also shown are aggregating mature caterpillars, aggregating early instar caterpillars in the shape resembling a spider and a group of chrysalises. The bottom right shows the lifecycle of the Speckled Line-blue butterfly that uses it as a host plant.
From the Butterfly Lives collection by Helen Schwencke

Trees   # *Butterflies*

Native Mulberry   ## *Jezebel Nymph*

Pipturus argenteus   *Mynes geoffroyi*

On many a morning Helen opens her door to a large female Native Mulberry that is often full of fruit and hears the quiet chatter of some Scaly-breasted Lorikeet busily having a meal. This is, for her, one of the many delights of the Native Mulberry, a smorgasbord for biodiversity, which often shows evidence of use by a wide variety of creatures.

The leaves feed two butterflies, the Jezebel Nymph (*Mynes geoffroyi*) in some years, and the Speckled Line-blue (*Catopyrops florinda*) highly reliably, along with the larvae of some species of Hawk Moth. Native mulberry also attracts other insects such as lacewings, grasshoppers and beetles, as well as many smaller spiders

While the flowers of both the female and male trees appear not to be attractive to insects, the female plants bear tiny, white, mulberry-like edible fruit that attract a range of fruit-eating birds. Even in the inner-Brisbane area, with its limited bird diversity, the tree routinely supports Scaly-breasted (*Trichoglossus chlorolepidotus*) and Rainbow Lorikeets (*Trichoglossus moluccanus*) and the ubiquitous Noisy Miners (*Manorina melanocephala*). Helen has observed a Crested Hawk (*Aviceda subcristata*) visiting one for a few days at a time, returning for several years, most likely to feed on the Giant Hedge grasshoppers (*Valanga irregularis*) that eat the leaves of the tree.

As a rainforest pioneer species, in its natural habitat the Native Mulberry grows at the forest edge and starts dying out when other plants overshadow it. It is fast-growing to around 6m and has very soft timber, so is easy to prune if required, and happily shoots back from severely pruned trunks. Female trees can start bearing their fruit from their first year. All these features make them suitable for smaller gardens. They can be a good shade tree, or can be thinned to whatever are your requirements.

Caper White
Belenois java

wingspan
55mm

♀

Scrub Caper
Capparis arborea

other butterflies:

Caper Gull

Striated
Pearl-white

© photos by Helen Schwencke & Frank Jordan, 2009   **www.earthling.com.au**   © Earthling Enterprises, 2019
plant photo © Trish Gardner, 2009

Scrub Caper, showing flowers and buds, with the lifecycle of the Caper White butterfly, as well as the adults of two of the other three butterflies that use it as a host plant. The top half shows the closed wing colouration of two of the three colour forms of the adults, and an open-winged adult female, as well as caterpillars and chrysalises. At rest, it is the closed wing presentation that is seen most frequently.
From the Butterfly Lives collection by Helen Schwencke

Scrub caper

Capparis arborea

Caper White

Belenois java

Practically every year, somewhere on the eastern seaboard there are reports of a migration of masses of white butterflies, with yellow and black markings. These Caper White butterflies (*Belenois java*) set out in spring, often in their millions, flying in a north-easterly direction, from their breeding grounds west of the Great Dividing Range, over the range to coastal areas of south-east Queensland and northern New South Wales looking for new sources of food to continue their life cycles.

On their way, the butterflies lay clutches of 40 or so eggs at a time on the fresh young growth of any of the three host species of caper bushes they can find. As the caterpillars hatch and start feeding, it is not unusual to see more exposed host plants stripped bare of their leaves, though the plants always recover.

Later in summer, if you are observant, you will see a small scattering of Caper Whites flying in a south-westerly direction as they migrate back inland. More recently there have been cases of continued breeding into late autumn and winter reported in the Lockyer Valley.

Whenever there is a large population spike, the predators, parasitoids and diseases quickly follow. Towards the end of the migration it can be hard to find caterpillars or chrysalises that are either viable or alive. This phenomenon, observed closely, makes for a great study in population dynamics and population ecology.

The caper bush host plant, *Capparis arborea*, starts life as a very small, spiky, slow growing seedling or root sucker. The species has been extensively removed from its normal range in the region supposedly because of its spiky and thorny nature. Once it grows above 20cm in height, the plant starts throwing up long stems with thorns, and the trunk develops small bunches of spines. In a natural setting you will find small groves of this medium-sized tree to 8 metres.

Scrub Capers support four species of butterflies in the Macleay McPherson Overlap. They are the already described Caper White, Caper Gull (*Cepora perimale*), Striated Pearl-white (*Elodina parthia*) and Southern Pearl-white (*Elodina angulipennis*). All these species belong to a family of butterflies called the Whites and Yellows (Family Pieridae). The introduced Cabbage White butterfly (*Pieris rapae*), the scourge of many gardeners' cabbages, also belongs to this family, so it is possible that the predators, parasitoids and diseases that attack the Caper Whites may also attack the Cabbage Whites. It could well be worth your while to include this tree in your plantings, both to harvest the edible flower buds or fruit, as well to build a reservoir of ally insects and diseases for any brassicas that you are growing in your garden.

The fruits of native caper bushes are tasty when ripe, and the pickled buds and the berries are reported to be tastier than the Mediterranean variety.

Other host plants in the region include: Bambul (*Capparis mitchellii*) (dry coastal and inland), *C. lasiantha* (drylands), *C. sarmentosa* (a prickly climber) and *C. velutina*. *Capparis sarmentosa* may be a good addition to plantings of dense prickly hedges mentioned in Section 4, Wildlife Friendly Gardening.

Tailed Emperor
Polyura sempronius

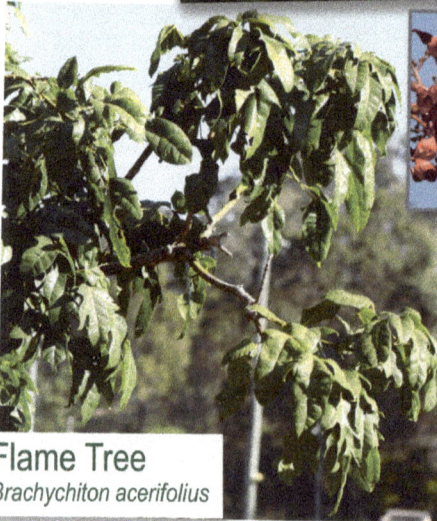

wingspan:
75 – 85mm

other butterfly:
White-banded Plane

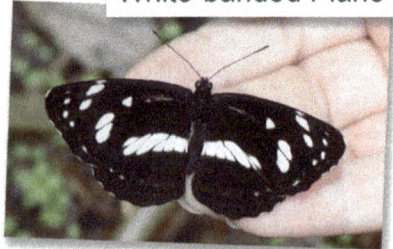

Flame Tree
Brachychiton acerifolius

© photos by Helen Schwencke, 2015   **www.earthling.com.au**   © Earthling Enterprises, 2015

Flame Tree, including an inset of its flowers, with the Tailed Emperor and White-banded Plane butterflies that use this plant as a host plant. The top half shows the lifecycle of the Tailed Emperor, with a caterpillar (which can have variable numbers of bands), a chrysalis (which is often not on the host plant), and adults, with both open and closed wings. The adult butterflies are most frequently seen when resting with wings closed.   *From the Butterfly Lives collection by Helen Schwencke*

Flame tree

Brachychiton acerifolius

Tailed Emperor

Polyura sempronius

Flame trees have been planted throughout southeast Queensland as street and park trees and their bright orange flowers are spectacular in late spring, especially on those trees that drop all their leaves before they flower.

A large tree growing to 30m. If you have the space, you could consider growing it as a scaffolding tree for a number of vines and scramblers that can benefit from its deciduous nature.

This tree is a host for three species of butterflies: the Tailed Emperor (*Polyura sempronius*), the White-banded Plane (*Phaedyma sherherdi*) and the Glistening or Common Pencil-blue (*Candalides absimilis*). Caterpillars of the Tailed Emperor and the White-banded Plane are spectacular in their own right.

White-banded Plane caterpillars are able to feed inconspicuously on their host plants because they are well-camouflaged against the debris field of the leaves they have chewed in a very specific pattern. The butterflies are black with white dots around the edges of their wings and have a floating and flitting flight pattern that is easy to identify and a delight to watch.

When examining the leaves of flame trees, there is often evidence that they are well used by a range of other species, which suggests that they may also host predator and parasitoid species that we find helpful in our gardens.

The seeds of flame trees are edible but you have to rub off their irritant yellow coating first, using a gloved hand. They can be eaten raw or roasted and taste like sunflower seeds. They also have a range of useful pharmacological properties[25].

A fun fact about Tailed Emperors is that this butterfly gets drunk on rotting fruit and fermenting sap. Despite having spectacular colour patterns on its outside wings, this butterfly is often hard to see because it is extremely flighty, flying fast and high. However, once drunk, it becomes very laid-back and is easy to photograph and observe. You can encourage this by leaving out some mashed banana mixed with beer. It does them no apparent harm.

White-banded Planes also use Koda (*Ehretia acuminata*) as a host plant where it occurs in or near creeklines. Koda is a smaller tree that grows from 6 to 10 metres tall and bears edible fruit that are small but sweet. They are eaten by a number of birds including Scaly-breasted Lorikeets.

White-banded Plane caterpillar
Helen Schwencke

White-banded Plane chrysalises, two colour forms.
Helen Schwencke

Scaly-breasted lorikeet feeding on Koda fruit   Frank Jordan

Bright Cornelian
Deudorix diovis

♂

wingspan:
30 - 31mm

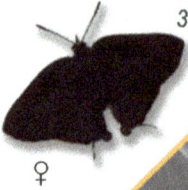

♀

other butterfly:
Common Pencilled-blue

Macadamia
Macadamia integrifolia

© photos by Helen Schwencke, 2015
& Frank Jordan

www.earthling.com.au

© Earthling Enterprises, 2015

Macadamia, with the caterpillars (upper picture), chrysalises (lower picture) and adults of the Bright Cornelian and Common Pencilled-blue butterflies, which use this plant as a host. The Bright Cornelian caterpillar is usually not visible as it grows inside the nut.

From the Butterfly Lives collection by Helen Schwencke

Macadamia

Bright Cornelian

Macadamia integrifolia

Deudorix diovis

It is with delight that Helen remembers many an hour spent at her father's bench vice working out how to apply just the right amount of pressure to crack a Queensland nut to release a perfect kernel, only to immediately eat it, or suffer the occasional disappointment of finding one that was shrivelled or otherwise occupied by a creature. Little did she understand then the amazing biodiversity that this plant supports while also remaining a productive food source.

Much later she learnt that one of the sources of shriveled kernels is the caterpillar of the Bright Cornelian butterfly (*Deudorix diovis*) which, long ago, adapted to making its livelihood by burrowing into newly forming seeds as a first instar caterpillar. She has since come to understand that this process is a natural form of biological control that, perhaps unwanted by us, makes sure that Macadamias do not form a monoculture. It is a small part of natural population control cycles.

Little needs to be said here about the uses for macadamias as a human food source. It is one of the few native Australian bush foods that has been commercialised.

Macadamias grow to around 8 metres high and are indigenous to South East Queensland rainforest. They are a host plant for six different species of butterflies all belonging to the Family Lycaenidae, known as the blues and coppers. The most conspicuous of these is the Bright Cornelian, the males of which have wings that are orange with a dark brown edge. The larvae of the other butterflies eat various parts of the plant, some the flowers and others, new leaves. The Common Pencilled-blue (*Candalides absimilis*) tip prunes new growth while the Large Purple Line-blue (*Nacaduba berenice*), the Short-tailed Line-blue (*Prosotas felderi*) and the Purple Line-blue (*Prosotas dubiosa*) all eat the flower buds and flowers, naturally controlling too much fruit set.

The biodiversity supported by the Macadamia extends to include the various species of ants that attend the butterfly larvae and increase their chances of survival. There is a whole range of other insects and other invertebrates, including a number of spiders as predators, that hang out in Macadamia trees. One of these insects is the native stingless bee *Tetragonula carbonaria*, which has adapted to pollinate plants in the Family Proteaceae, which includes Macadamia, and can increase the pollination rate to increase productivity by ten percent.

Some Large Purple Line-blue lifecycle stages. From LHS showing two colour forms of the caterpillars, a closed wing adult, female and male with open wings. Purple and blue colours on butterflies depend on how the light is refracted as it falls on the wings.   Helen Schwencke

Dainty Swallowtail
Papilio anactus

wingspan:
67 - 72mm

other butterflies:
Orchard Swallowtail

♂

♀

& Fuscous Swallowtail

Native Finger Lime
Citrus australasica

© photos by Helen Schwencke, 2017
& Glenn Leiper
www.earthling.com.au
© Earthling Enterprises, 2017
Dainty Swtwtl Citrus australasica v3-2 A4 lyr

Finger Lime, showing an inset of its fruit, which comes in yellow, green and dark red colour forms, with the lifecycle of the Dainty Swallowtail butterfly and the adults of the Orchard Swallowtail and the Fuscous Swallowtail, all of which use this plant as a host plant. The Dainty Swallowtail is shown in both closed and open wing views, with its caterpillar and chrysalis as well.

From the Butterfly Lives collection by Helen Schwencke

Shrubs

Butterflies

Finger Lime & Pink Limeberry

Dainty & Fuscous Swallowtail

Citrus australasica & Glycosmis trifoliata

Papilio anactus, P. fuscus

Finger Lime, a small native citrus, is host to the caterpillars of the Orchard Swallowtail (*Papilio aegeus*), Fuscous Swallowtail (*Papilio fuscus*) and Dainty Swallowtail (*Papilio anactus*) butterflies. In south east Queensland, it is the most reliable host plant for the Dainty Swallowtail's caterpillars. Finger Lime is a popular native food plant, and there are many delicious ways of using its colourful fruit in drinks, garnishes, sauces, sweets and jams.

Growing to a height of only 2 to 4m, and with a compact growth habit, it can fit into smaller gardens and spaces. It is very prickly and can be quite dense, so it can provide protection and nesting places for smaller birds such as finches and wrens in suburban settings. As most Australian birds need to feed insects to their young, providing a nesting place for these birds will help control any population explosions of insects in your garden.

Finger Lime is a member of the Rutaceae Family of plants, which also includes a number of other native plants, as well as introduced citrus such as oranges, lemons, limes, mandarins. They all host one or more of these three butterflies. Introduced citrus can attract Orchard Swallowtail butterflies, and their caterpillars can damage and even overwhelm smaller plants, but on bigger plants their chewing of leaves is seldom a problem.

A native plant in the Rutaceae family, the Pink Lime berry is a reliable host for the Fuscous Swallowtail in south-east Queensland, even though the plant's original range was slightly to the north. It grows to 4m and has small pink fruit which have an interesting flavour.

The chrysalis of the Fuscous Swallowtail can remain in a state of suspended animation, called diapause, for at least two years if necessary, as a way of surviving droughts and seasons of poor growth. Diapause is a strategy used by many insect species: their pupae emerge in numbers when conditions become conducive to continuing their life cycles.

Citrus trees, both introduced and native, also support many other invertebrates. A field guide to spiders in Brisbane that was published in 1996 documented 48 spider species that were supported by citrus trees in orchards. (Green, J. Field Guide to Spiders [Brisbane], Cooperative Research Centre for Tropical Pest Management and Department of Entomology, The University of Queensland, 1996)

Pink Limeberry in fruit.
Helen Schwencke

Fuscous Swallowtail caterpillars LHS - the green one on top is ready to pupate - and RHS a chrysalis.
Helen Schwencke

Eastern Dusk-flat
Chaetocneme beata

wingspan:
47 - 52mm

Bolwarra
Eupomatia laurina

© photos by Helen Schwencke, 2015 **www.earthling.com.au** © Earthling Enterprises, 2015
& Glenn Leiper for flower inset, © Shanna Bignell for the main open-wing butterfly image

Bolwarra, showing an inset of its flowers and buds with a ripening fruit, and the lifecycle of the Eastern Dusk-flat butterfly. The three smaller images on the left show, from the bottom, a chrysalis, a mature caterpillar (both usually hidden in a shelter), and the shelter the new caterpillar makes soon after hatching from an egg. This butterfly settles in the open wing position. At the top left is a male butterfly, and the main image is a female. From the Butterfly Lives collection by Helen Schwencke

Long-leaved Bolwarra

Eupomatia laurina

Eastern Dusk-flat

Chaetocneme beata

Bolwarra, with its beautiful glossy leaves, and weeping growth habit, is a shrub that grows to 5m in the shady understory of rainforest, mostly near creeklines. The ripe fruit is edible and makes a delicious liqueur, as crafted by John and Mary King of Rainforest Liqueurs.

Bolwarra is a host for the Eastern Dusk-flat (*Chaetocneme beata*) and you will know if you have the butterfly caterpillar when you see the little shelter it makes by cutting out a piece of the leaf and curling it over. It lives in this shelter for at least the first two instars and, as it grows, it makes a shelter out of two leaves that it stitches together. It also pupates in this shelter. The butterfly can sometimes be found sheltering under leaves during the day and it can also be attracted to lights at night.

This ancient flowering plant relies for its pollination on rainforest weevils (*Elleschodes* spp) so you do not get fruit to set without this weevil. Helen has also occasionally found colonies of Stick-insects on this plant, Tessellated Stick-insects (*Anchiale austrotessulata*) at Mt Nebo, and an unidentified Stick-insect (possibly a nymph of a Dark-winged Stick-insect *(Mesaner sarpedon)* at Binna Burra.

Joseph's Coat Moth
Agarista agricola

♀

wingspan:
50mm

♂

♀

♂

other species:
Cruria donowani

a beetle:
Oides dorsosignata

Slender Grapevine or Native Grape
Cayratia clematidea

© photos by Helen Schwencke, 2015   **www.earthling.com.au**   © Earthling Enterprises, 2015

*Slender Grapevine, showing an inset of its flowers, and the lifecycle of the day-flying Joseph's Coat Moth, along with images of two of the other species that use this host plant: the beetle **Oides dorsosignata**, and the caterpillar and adult of the day-flying moth **Cruria donowani**. The images of the Joseph's Coat moth from top LHS show the fairly subtle difference in the underside wings of both the female and the male. Across the middle are the open wings of the female and the male moths, and on the LHS are a caterpillar and the pupal shelter (usually hidden in the leaf litter). This moth settles in the open wing position.   From the Butterfly Lives collection by Helen Schwencke*

Vines and Scramblers

Slender Grape Vine

Cayratia clematidea

Butterflies

Joseph's Coat Moth

Agarista agricola

Slender Grape vine is a graceful climbing plant, with an ornamental leaf shape, that can grow vigorously, its weak stems extending to 2m or more. Unfortunately, to an untrained eye, it can be easily mistaken for an introduced invasive species, Balloon Vine (*Cardiospermum grandiflorum*), and is sometimes removed as such.

Slender Grape vine is a pioneer species found along rainforest edges and in clearings, sometimes covering other understorey vegetation. However, we have yet to see one that has not been rapidly defoliated by the caterpillars of a number of moths, including one or more of the ten species of Hawkmoths recorded for south-east Queensland, the spectacular Joseph's coat moth (*Agarista agricola*) or, less frequently, a day-flying, black and white moth, *Cruria donowani*. Its leaves are also eaten by the orange and black *Oides dorsosignata* beetle and its larvae.

The vine usually dies back in the cooler months and resprouts from underground tubers, so if you plant this species you will have it to stay, unless you decide to harvest and cook the tubers. These are described as edible although lacking in flavour. The fruit, when black and ripe, is edible, though also lacking in flavour, and is food for fruit eating birds that will also distribute the seeds.

Let us know if this host plant remains as a large plant in your area, and doesn't die off in winter.

Pale Triangle
Graphium eurypylus

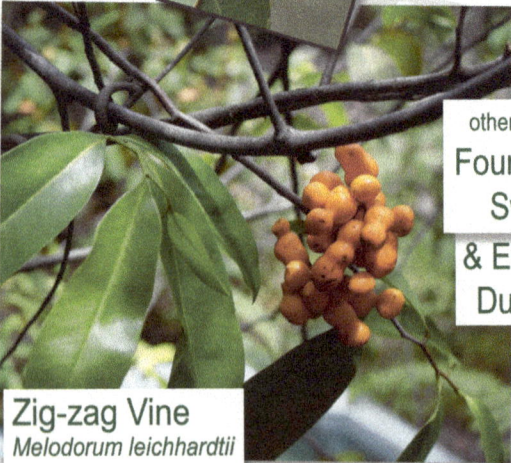

wingspan:
59 - 62mm

other butterflies:
Four-barred Swordtail
& Eastern Dusk-flat

Zig-zag Vine
Melodorum leichhardtii

© photos by Helen Schwencke, 2009   www.earthling.com.au   © Earthling Enterprises, 2010
butterfly images © Todd Burrows (open wings), © Stephen Noble (side view)

Zig-zag Vine, showing its leaves and fruit. Note how its stems loop around themselves. The different stages of the lifecycle of the Pale Triangle include three caterpillar instars that are markedly different in colour, the camouflaged chrysalis and the adult butterfly, shown with both open and closed wings. The adults of two of the other species that use this host plant, the Four-bar Swordtail and the Eastern Dusk-flat, are also shown, in the bottom right hand side.

From the Butterfly Lives collection by Helen Schwencke

Zig Zag Vine

Melodorum leichhardtii

Pale Triangle

Graphium eurypylus

Zig Zag vine is one of those rare treasures of a bush food, with fruit that is tangy, sweet and delectable, perhaps unsurprisingly as it is related to custard apple and soursop.

It is a scrambler that climbs its way through scaffolding trees and other vegetation in rainforests and dry vine forests. Left to its own devices, and with nothing to climb up, it grows as a shrub like plant with dense foliage and it is also possible to prune it into this growth habit. Young plants are very slow growing for the first few years, so you need patience, but you will be well rewarded.

The plant supports the caterpillars of two of the larger Australian butterflies in the Swallowtail family, namely the Four-barred Swordtail (*Protographium leosthenes*) and the Pale Triangle (*Graphium eurypylus*). It also supports the Eastern Dusk-flat (*Chaetocneme beata*). Pale Triangle butterflies are known for their variation in the colour of their markings, from blackish with custard-like yellow, through pale green to pale blue.

This is a bush food and habitat plant that lends itself to being grown in food gardens. It could also be used as an addition to dense hedge plantings, to add foliage for the protection of small birds.

♂
wingspan:
28 - 29mm

♀

♂

Indigo Flash
Rapala varuna

Millaa Millaa Vine
Elaeagnus triflora

© photos by Helen Schwencke, 2015   **www.earthling.com.au**   © Earthling Enterprises, 2020
and © Dick Copeman for the image of the main butterfly with closed wings

Millaa Millaa vine (at the bottom), showing a ripe and unripe fruit, and giving a glimpse at the silvery to coppery undersides of the leaves. Also illustrated is the lifecycle of the Indigo Flash butterfly. The caterpillar and chrysalis are shown at the bottom RHS and the main image shows the adult butterfly settled in its normal, closed wing position, where it is often seen wriggling the false antennae and eye-spots at its hind end. The three smaller images on the left show, from the bottom, a closed wing male butterfly, and an open-winged female and male. The wing colour is the result of a refraction pattern and depends on the angle at which the photo was taken.

From the Butterfly Lives collection by Helen Schwencke

Millaa Millaa Vine

Elaeagnus triflora

Indigo Flash

Rapala varuna

The leaves of Millaa Millaa, with their shiny copper or silver undersides, are a delight to behold as they shimmer in a light breeze. This plant is a vigorous climber of tropical and subtropical rainforests, with a sprawling habit and shoots up to 8m long. It normally climbs through other vegetation but can be kept pruned as a shrub.

The Atlas of Living Australia records its distribution from north Queensland south to the New South Wales border area. It makes a beautiful, though less brightly colour- ed, substitute for bougainvillaea and has the added advantages of not being prickly and of bearing a delicious fruit. This slowly changes colour from green through various lovely intermediate shades to a beautiful red colour when ripe.

The small and insignificant flowers are the first meals of early instar caterpillars of a small but bright butterfly, the Indigo Flash (*Rapala varuna*). The more mature cater- pillars eat the young leaves. If you see males of this butterfly on the wing, you will see that its name is justified.

The Indigo Flash has a number of other recorded host plants but does not appear to use many of them reliably. One that has been used is the introduced Loquat tree (*Eriobotica japonica*), a common backyard fruit tree with sweet, tangy fruit. The caterpillar eats the maturing fruit. Unfortunately, in the Brisbane area, these are no longer setting much fruit, as winter nights have become warmer, but they are still fruiting in areas with cooler nights.

wingspan:
50mm

Yellow Admiral
Vanessa itea

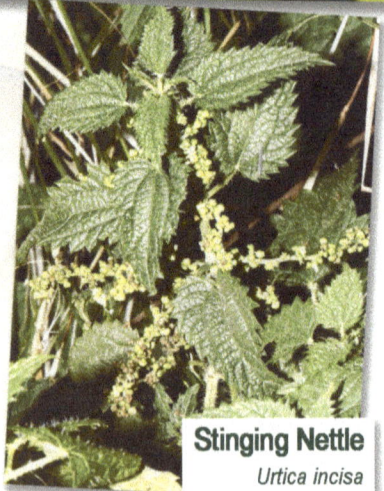

Stinging Nettle
Urtica incisa

© photos by Helen Schwencke, 2020   **www.earthling.com.au**   © Earthling Enterprises, 2020
and © Jacob Krijt for the main butterfly image and Rob Macaulay for outline view

Stinging Nettle, showing spent flowers, and the stinging hairs that give the plant its name, as well as the lifecycle of the Yellow Admiral butterfly that the plant supports. From the bottom LHS moving around to the top are the images of a chrysalis and caterpillar (both of which can have different colour forms), an open wing image of the butterfly seen when the butterfly is sunning itself, and a closed wing image which is the position it frequently settles. The caterpillar image also shows a caterpillar in a curled up leaf, which is where they are most frequently found.

From the Butterfly Lives collection by Helen Schwencke

Ground Covers

Stinging Nettle

Urtica incisa

Butterflies

Yellow Admiral

Vanessa itea

Native Stinging Nettle may not be the most obvious choice of a food plant we can share. You will need to choose the location for growing this ground-covering herb carefully, to avoid accidental encounters with its stinging hairs. It grows best in moist areas at the edge of rainforests or creeklines, where it can receive both sun and shade. You could try to grow it if you're considering putting in a soak area in your garden (see Section 4: Wildlife Friendly Gardening - Provide water).

Boiling, or careful and thorough wilting, inactivates the sting in the leaves, which can then be eaten as a nutritious dark green leafy vegetable or in soups. The native Australian species (*Urtica incisa*) is able to be used in any recipe that uses European nettles (*Urtica urens*).

The Yellow Admiral (*Vanessa itea*), a beautiful medium-sized butterfly, uses both species as caterpillar food plants. The caterpillars live in curled up leaves that they stitch lightly together with a little of their silk. When harvesting this plant for food, it is a good idea to check the leaves carefully to make sure you are not inadvertently also collecting caterpillars. Unchecked leaves may have you inadvertently eating some extra protein that was not on your menu!

Both the stationary butterfly when sitting, quietly undisturbed with its wings folded, as well as the chrysalis, are difficult to see as they resemble dried up nettle leaves. When you disturb the butterflies, they may raise their upper wing to reveal a blue-eyed spot, or fly off showing their lovely orange-brown, yellow and dark brown markings.

Chequered Swallowtail
Papilio demoleus

wingspan:
72 - 75mm

Emu Foot
Cullen tenax

© photos by Helen Schwencke, 2015   www.earthling.com.au   © Earthling Enterprises, 2015

Emu Foot, showing a broad-leaved form, supports the Chequered Swallowtail, with its lifecycle presented here. The smaller images at the top left show a chrysalis at the bottom and the colour variation of different instars of the caterpillars. The main image shows the adult butterfly with open wings, prepared for flight and the bottom right image shows a view of the underside of the open wings.

From the Butterfly Lives collection by Helen Schwencke

Emu Foot

Cullen tenax

Chequered Swallowtail

Papilio demoleus

This delicate looking, perennial ground cover arises from a single deep tap root and weaves its way through grasses and other vegetation as it grows and spreads.

It grows naturally in dry sclerophyll forest but, in the past, it was sadly misrepresented as a weed of neglected lawns. It is an adaptable plant that is now considered good for stabilizing the soil, for bringing nutrients up to the topsoil from deeper layers, and as a nitrogen fixer.

Given a chance, this plant will grow thick and lush to a height of around 30 cm and spread out for about a metre, with runners that don't bear roots. This state may not last long as often, in November, Chequered Swallowtail butterflies (*Papilio demoleus*) will locate Emu Foot plants on their migration eastwards.

The females then lay little round eggs, which hatch within a few days into tiny caterpillars, which look like bird droppings for the first two or three instars, before changing to a rusty brown colour. The final instar is green with spots and a white stripe along the sides. The green pupa is well-camouflaged against the leaves and plant stalks and the adult Chequered Swallowtail butterfly that emerges is truly spectacular, and a fast flyer.

This plant also feeds the larvae of two other butterflies, the Common Grass-blue (*Zizina labradus*), and the Tailed Pea-blue (*Lampides boeticus*), the latter of which has adapted to also feeding on some of our introduced legume food crops. So having Emu Foot on hand may lead to there being more predators, and other control agents being available for your crops. Try it out and see.

The tiny pink to purple flowers of the Emu Foot produce little black seeds, which are fragrant when roasted and can be used as a substitute for poppy seed in cooking and baking. It is thought that Cullen tenax can self-pollinate to a large degree.

Evening Brown
Melanitis leda

wingspan:
60 - 63mm

dry season
form

wet season
form

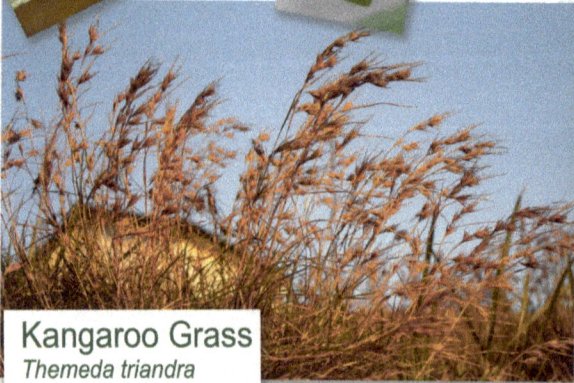

wet season
form

Kangaroo Grass
Themeda triandra

© photos by Helen Schwencke, 2016   **www.earthling.com.au**   © Earthling Enterprises, 2016

Kangaroo Grass, shown catching the evening sun at Cape Moreton, with an inset of the seed heads in normal daylight. Also showing the lifecycle of the Evening Brown butterfly, for which Kangaroo grass is a host plant. From the middle centre, moving around to the left and upwards are: a chrysalis, a two-horned caterpillar, the closed wing images of a wet and dry season adult, and a dry season form of the open-winged adult. The main image is of a wet season adult. The butterfly normally settles with its wings closed.

From the Butterfly Lives collection by Helen Schwencke

Kangaroo Grass

Themeda triandra

Evening Brown

Melanitis leda

Walk through a patch of tall grasses in an open woodland, on dusk, and you are likely to be startled by a fairly large brown butterfly, the Evening Brown (*Melanitis leda*). It will fly off, then land quickly and be so completely hidden that you will have a really hard time finding it unless you saw exactly where it landed. Kangaroo grass, a common woodland grass throughout Australia, is a host plant for the Evening Brown as well as nine other species of butterfly. Its weeping growth habit, reddish colour in certain lightings, and distinctive seed heads make it a lovely garden addition. It is a perennial grass that grows to about 1.5m tall in a tussock about half a metre wide and can be grown ornamentally in rockeries or other locations in your garden. As with all grasses, it is wind-pollinated.

With several Kangaroo Grass plants in your garden, you can attract Evening Brown butterflies and at least some of the other smaller butterflies that it hosts. This potentially makes it a great biodiversity enhancer. Their caterpillars will eat the leaves while you can harvest the seed. It was used by the First Australians to make damper for many thousands of years and moves are afoot by indigenous Australians to bring it back into cultivation and use as a drought tolerant and gluten free grain.

Evening Browns have two other host plants, and both have edible parts. One is Blady Grass (*Imperata cylindrica*), whose rhizomes can be eaten raw while tender shoots and young flowers can be cooked. The other is the very pretty, aromatic, Barb-wire Grass (*Cymbopogon refractus*) which is known as native lemongrass. It can be used as a citrus-like flavouring in cooking or made into a tea.

Meadow Argus
Junonia villida

wingspan:
40 - 43 mm

Shade Plantain
Plantago debilis

© photos by Helen Schwencke, 2009
& Frank Jordan   **www.earthling.com.au**   © Earthling Enterprises, 2009

Shade Plantain, with partly spent seed heads and some new flower spikes, supports the Meadow Argus butterfly's lifecycle as illustrated. From centre bottom to top showing a chrysalis, caterpillar, and the closed wings side view. The main image shows the open-winged adult sipping on the nectar of a paper daisy flower. This is the most common view of this butterfly as it patrols open ground and alights on plants.
From the Butterfly Lives collection by Helen Schwencke

Shade Plantain

Plantago debilis

Meadow Argus

Junonia villida

A lovely sight in early summer is male Meadow Argus (*Junonia villida*) butterflies patrolling patches of meadow or open fields. In the right light, these butterflies shimmer a coppery colour.

One of the host plants for these butterflies is the native ground cover, Shade Plantain. This broad-leaved herb grows as a rosette from a single tap root, with its deeply veined leaves spreading out for about 20cm and its flower spike growing to about the same height.

The young leaves of plantains are edible. While the caterpillars are frequently visible on the leaves that they are eating, it is a good idea to check these carefully if you are harvesting them. The seeds can be used to make a drink that thickens up naturally, or boiled water can be added to make a sago-like dessert. This plant is related to an introduced Plantago that is used to produce psyllium husks.

The Meadow Argus butterfly also uses a number of other edible species as host plants, including introduced plantains that are common garden weeds in some areas, as well as the pigweeds, *Portulaca australis* (a native) and *P. oleracea* (introduced). If you would like a host plant with some pretty flowers, then grow the ground-covering Fan-flower (*Scaevola aemula*) or the short, upright, damp soil loving Centaury (*Schenkia australis*). When in flower, the native Centaury has been observed by Helen to be also very popular with native stingless bees (*Tetragonula carbonaria*).

6. Ecological strategies to control common garden 'pests'

The discussion that led to the creation of this book started between the two of us, and a few other members of the Queensland Naturalists' Club, on an excursion to a property on the Darling Downs in 2015. We were looking at a garden plot that included a long row of kale plants being grown in ground that was kept bare of other plants by mulching. All the while we were watching Cabbage White butterflies coming and laying their eggs.

Kale plants, looking a little stressed. Though they grow well in the humid subtropics, thay are more suited to a cool temperate climate.
Dick Copeman

The ecologist in us realised that, while this is standard plant cultivation practice, there are few situations in nature where plants grow with only other plants of the same species. Such practice allows the butterflies to more easily locate a food source as they are cued in to the smell of the plant and find it more easily in bare ground. Once a food source is located, with no reservoirs of predators, parasitoids and diseases nearby, and with each butterfly capable of laying up to 400 eggs, it is a recipe for a small scale population explosion of the butterfly and its caterpillars. The result that most gardeners are familiar with is that there is little kale left to eat after the caterpillars have had their fill.

As a general principle of nature, this practice creates an "island" of food with little other life in it. Nature abhors a vacuum, so sooner or later something will come and eat it. Helen has frequently observed this phenomenon while growing a few isolated potted herbs on her window sill. Sooner or later, one or other creature finds its way to the plants and starts an "infestation". When she relocates the plant into a group of other, mostly native, plants in pots, in most cases, a day or two later the herbivores are gone and her herbs are re-shooting.

There are two possible explanations of this observation. Either the other native plants are directly supporting predators, parasitoids or diseases that keep in check the insects that are damaging Helen's herb by providing food or habitat for them, or they are indirectly attracting the predators parasitoids and diseases by hosting other herbivorous insects that are closely related to the insect that is eating Helen's herb, the assumption being that closely related insects attract the same or similar predators.

The first scenario has been widely adopted by organic gardeners and farmers and by practitioners of Integrated Pest Management in conventional farming, although mainly through planting exotic plants whose flowers support predators. The second scenario is more experimental: it sounds plausible in theory but we can find no evidence that it has been proven or disproven, or even tried, in practice.

So we are suggesting two main ecological control strategies for the insect herbivores that can eat our food crops:

- Grow other, local, native plants that host the predators, parasitoids or diseases nearby so that your preferred plants have ready access to a potential reservoir of predators, parasitoids and diseases that can transfer to your plants and help control excessive damage by the herbivores. This is the tried and true strategy.

- Grow other, local native, plants nearby that are the host plants for closely related insect herbivores, in the hope that these related herbivores will attract predators, parasitoids and diseases that will also utilise the herbivore that is eating your plants. This is the experimental strategy, more details of which are below in the discussion about Cabbage White caterpillars.

These ecological control strategies are both 'no regrets' strategies in that both contribute to the more general project of reintroducing as much local native vegetation as possible into our gardens as a way of reconstructing biodiverse landscapes to help reduce species losses, starting with herbivorous insects which are at the base of food webs, as was described in Section 3.

What follows are some specific examples of ecological solutions for just some of the common insect 'pest' problems, ecologically speaking our competitor species, that are encountered by gardeners.

Lepidoptera

- ## *Cabbage white caterpillar (Pieris rapae) - Family Pieridae.*

   The small, deep green caterpillars of this introduced butterfly eat the leaves of all members of the cabbage or Brassica family, including broccoli, cauliflower and kale. Many of these varieties of vegetables are cultivars of the same species, a plant that this butterfly originally evolved with in its place of origin.

   Growing flowering plants amongst, or near, your Brassicas will provide nectar that can help attract predatory wasps of two sorts, the larger paper wasps (*Polistes* spp.) that capture the cater-

*This image is still taken from a video of a paper wasp, possibly **Polistes humilis synoecus**, that carefully and systematically "butchered" the caterpillar. The pieces of the caterpillar were collected into a ball to be delivered to its nest to feed the next generation of wasps.*
Amelia Pasieczny

A Geometrid moth caterpillar in which a parasitoid Ichneumon wasp has laid its eggs. The wasp larvae have emerged from the eggs and spun silk cocoons in which to pupate. The black hole near the middle of the image is the hole through which one or more of the wasp larvae have emerged. A small unidentified wasp is visible on the cocoons. Caterpillars like this that are found on a "bed" of wasp pupae do not survive.   Beth Cavallari

A Black Tip Band-winged Braconid Wasp (Iphiaulax danielsi) freshly emerged from the pupal shelter of a Joseph's Coat Moth raised by Helen. See page 60-61. There are an estimated 800 or more species of Braconid wasps in Australia. Some are external, others internal parasites of a wide range of insects. Some are specific to a single or small range of hosts; others are more generalist in what they can use as a food source for their larvae.
Helen Schwencke

A dead Speckled Line-blue butterfly pupa (see page 48-49) showing a large hole that was made by a Tachinid fly larva as it left to form a pupa of its own. The over 500 species of Australian Tachinid flies utilise many other insects and invertebrates as their larval food supply.
Helen Schwencke

pillars to feed their larvae, and smaller Braconid wasps (Cotesia spp.) that parasitise the cabbage white caterpillars directly.

Another possible, but experimental, bio-control for Cabbage White caterpillars would be to plant the Scrub Caper (Capparis arborea), which is host plant for the Caper White (Belenois java), Caper Gull (Cepora perimale), Striated Pearl-White (Elod-ina parthia), and the Southern Pearl-white (Elodina angulipennis), all local native butterflies that are related to the introduced Cabbage White. These Whites and Pearl-whites, attracted by the Caper, would attract predators, parasitoids and diseases that may also help control the Cabbage White cater-pillars. See also Section 5 for more information about Native Capers and their butterflies.

- **Corn earworm and native budworm - caterpillars of Helicoverpa (formerly Heliothis) moth spp. (Family: Noctuidae)**

These large brown caterpillars can consume considerable amounts of the flowers and fruit of tomatoes, corn, sunflowers, beans, pigeon pea and citrus. Providing native plant habitats for predatory bugs, predatory beetles, spiders, lacewings, ants, parasitoid wasps, tachinid flies, and pathogenic viruses can help control populations of these caterpillars. [26, 27]

- **Fruit piercing moths - Eudocima spp.) (Family: Erebidae)**

The adult moths feed on carambola, banana, citrus, fig, guava, kiwifruit, longan lychee, mango, stone fruit, persimmon and ripening papaya. Larval hosts include native vines of the Family Menispermaceae, with the common Tape Vine (Stephania japonica) the main one in SE QLD and N NSW, so growing these trees away from native bush can reduce the risk of damage to fruit. As an example of population cycles discussed earlier in Section 3, late summer and early autumn of 2020 was an exceptional year for high population numbers of these moths.

Several native wasps are known to parasitise larvae of these moths but have limited impact during summer.[28] Increasing the population of insectivorous micro-bats by providing suitable roosting sites may also help but many of the tree hollows where these creatures once roosted have been removed.

- **Macadamia Nut Borer (Larva of the moth, Cryptophlebia ombrodelta)**

    This caterpillar eats lychee and longan fruit, as well as macadamias.

    The egg parasitoid, *Trichgrammatoidea cryptophlebiae*, which is a native of Africa, has become established in Australia and provides excellent biological control of the macadamia nut borer, especially in longans later in summer. Numerous native larval parasites utilise the borer, including braconid and ichneumonid wasps, and at least one tachinid fly parasite[29], so grow flowering native plants nearby as a food source for these ally insects.

    For another, less problematic, competitor, the Bright Cornelian (*Deudorix diovis*) butterfly, the experimental approach, described above, could be tried. The caterpillars of this species are borers of the seeds of various native plants, Macadamias amongst them. A related butterfly species, the Indigo Flash (*Rapala varuna*), has the Millaa Millaa vine, (*Elaeagnus triflora*), as one of its host plants. By planting this nearby, you may support a reservoir of predatory and parasitoid insects that could help protect the Macadamia from this borer. The vine has delectable fruit, so you could also benefit from a side crop. See Section 5 for more details about hosts for the Indigo Flash butterfly.

*An unidentified Lynx spider (possibly an **Oxyopes** sp.) observed guarding an egg of a Swallowtail butterfly. Was it waiting for the caterpillar to hatch for a small high protein snack?   Teale Britstra*

*These Caper White butterfly eggs (see pages 28, 50-51), about 1mm long, have attracted the attention of an unidentified, and even smaller parasitoid wasp that can complete its whole lifecycle within one egg.
Teale Britstra*

*With the chewed leaf as evidence of its having had a recent meal, this early instar Common Crow caterpillar (**Euploea corinna**) itself became a meal for an unidentified ant and its colony. Ants from a wide range of species can be found patrolling plants and taking both live prey and insect eggs.   Annette Dexter*

Diptera

- **Queensland fruit fly (Bactrocera tryoni).**

    This native species affects a wide range of native and exotic fruits. The adult flies lay their eggs in the ripening fruit, which hatch into larvae or grubs that eat the fruit and also attract bacterial rots.

Parasitoids attack the pupae and can help reduce transmission from year to year, but are not effective once numbers of adults have built up. Non-chemical controls include removing fallen fruit, covering ripening fruit, as well as baits and traps.

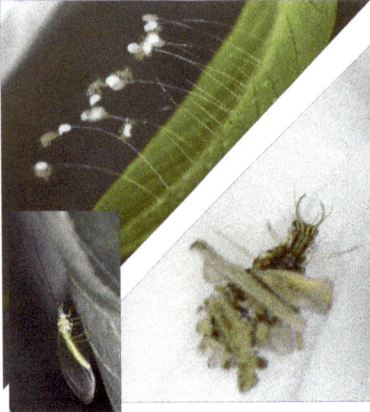

*Golden-eyed Green Lacewing eggs hatching (top) and a larva (bottom). As a disguise, the predatory larvae carry on their backs the skeletons of their prey or plant matter as in the image above. These Lacewings are very difficult to ID from images and belong to four different genera: **Apertochrysa** spp., **Mallada** spp., **Chrysoperla** spp. and **Plesiochrysa** spp. The images here may or may not be of the same species.*
Helen Schwencke

*A Garden Mantis **(Orthodera ministralis)** with an egg case, called an Ootheca that appears to be a type of hardened foam.*
Dick Copeman (mantis),
Helen Schwencke (ootheca)

Hemiptera

• *Aphids - Family Aphididae*

These are small sap-sucking insects that affect new growth of garden plants. They also transmit viruses and exude honeydew that attracts ants and encourages black sooty mould to grow. There are very few native species of aphids, and those that are, have very specific host plant relationships. The aphids that affect our food plants have been introduced along with their plants.

Their natural enemies include the larvae of lacewings, hover flies and lady beetles, some lady beetle adults, and parasitic wasps.

• *Whitefly - Family Aleyrodidae*

Whitefly are small, moth-like, sucking insects that aggregate in large numbers under plant leaves and utilise a wide range of food plants, including tomatoes and beans. They cause yellowing, leaf loss, wilting and stunting and, like aphids, exude honeydew that attracts ants and black sooty mould.

Predators of whiteflies include spiders, lady-bird larvae, lacewings, hoverflies, damsel bugs, parasitoid wasps, predatory mites and predatory bugs, and they can all contribute to the control of explosions of whitefly populations. A parasitic wasp, *Encarsia formosa*, is commercially available as a biological control and it is possible to achieve good results without resorting to chemical treatments[30].

• *Mealy bugs - Family Pseudococcidae*

These fluffy white insects suck the sap from citrus, custard apples and other subtropical fruit trees.

Predators include parasitoid wasps and lady beetle adults and larvae, including one common species, the Mealybug Ladybird (*Cryptolaemus montrouzieri*), whose larvae mimic mealy bugs.

• *Scale insects - Super Family Coccoidea*

These are small round, immobile insects that are often found along the veins on the undersides of leaves, and on bark. They are sap suckers and can weaken and even kill smaller trees.

Their predators include parasitic wasps such as *Aphytis melinus*, ladybirds, esp. *Chilocorus* and *Rhyzobius* spp., lacewings, hover flies, caterpillars of some moths (*Mataeomera* spp., (some sources spell the genus name as *Metaeomera*)) and insectivorous birds[31].

• *Fruit spotting bug (Amblypelta nitida)*

These affect commercial crops of many subtropical and tropical fruits, including avocados, macadamias, custard apples, lychee, passionfruit, pawpaw, citrus, bananas and mango in particular. They can also affect fruit in home gardens, causing premature fruit drop, lesions in the fruit and tree dieback.

You can help reduce fruit spotting bug numbers by encouraging predators including assassin bugs, spiders, ants, lacewings and general vertebrate predators such as birds and frogs. Many wasps are parasitoids of fruit spotting bug eggs, while various Tachinid flies parasitise the nymphs and adults[32]

Fruit spotting bug is more of a problem in areas adjacent to bushland that contains native host plants such as silver quandong, tuckeroo and beach alectryon, especially if there are few understorey plants to provide habitat for predators and parasitoids.

*Mealybug Ladybird (**Cryptolaemus montrouzieri**) life-cycle, showing larva (top LHS), three pupae (bottom RHS) and adult.*   Helen Schwencke

*Yellow-shouldered Hover fly, probably a female **Ischiodon scutellaris**, resting on a random leaf. When flying, some of the members of this large group of flies can stay stationary, or appear to move forwards and backwards in a darting motion.*   Erica Siegel

*A Northern Green Jumping Spider (**Mopus mormon**), female, stalking (top) and then catching (bottom) an unidentified juvenile sap-sucking bug obscured, in part, by the leaf.*   Helen Schwencke

*Golden Orb weaver spider (**Nephila** sp., probably **N. edulis**) with a grasshopper meal, and with evidence of previous meals.*   *Annette Dexter*

*An unidentified Robber Fly, possibly one of those described as short-winged, **Bathy-pogon** sp. It was attracted to a UV emitting light at night. Robber flies are voracious predators.*   *Helen Schwencke*

For a fascinating read about the role of mites, domatia and predatory mites, see the article by Dave Walter, "Little Houses in Big Trees" in Wildilfe Australia, Autumn 2017, pp. 26 - 31

Planting a diverse range of native shrubs around and amongst orchards provides predator habitat as well as a physical barrier to the fruit spotting bugs.[33]

Orthoptera

• Grasshoppers - Sub-order Caelifera

Birds are the most important predators of grasshoppers, so provide trees, shrubs, water and food to attract birds to your garden. See page 49 for a description of a Crested Hawk preying on Giant Hedge Grasshoppers in Helen's garden.

Other creatures that prey on grasshoppers include lizards, spiders and predatory carabid and rove beetles, and insects such as paper wasps, tachinid flies, parasitic wasps and robber flies.[34]

Other Invertebrates
Arachnida

• Spider mite - Family Tetranychidae

These tiny spider-like creatures colonise the underside of leaves, where they puncture plant cells to feed on the contents. Signs of their presence include stippling visible on the upper surface of the leaf, dry-ing up of the leaves and a fine silken webbing under the leaves.

Natural control agents include lacewings, tiny mite-feeding ladybirds, predatory gall-midges and a variety of predatory mites. Predatory mites live in domatia, small pits on the back of the leaves of some native plants such as the Rose Walnut (Endiandra dis-color), a tall tree, and Native Grapes (Cissus spp), so that planting these species may bring the predatory mites that could help control spider mite infestations.

Molluscs

- ## *Common Brown Garden Snail (Helix aspersa)*

  The snails that are the most damaging to our food plants are introduced species. Australia has many thousands of endemic species of snail, which have particular and highly specialised ecological roles.

  One method of control for the Common Brown Garden Snail (*Helix aspersa*) is to use them as a food source as they are edible. Another method is to encourage Blue Tongue lizards (*Tiliqua* spp) by providing ground covers and other places where they can hide while visiting your garden. You need to leave their trails through your garden. They may also take a chomp out of a strawberry while passing by but they are wonderful for controlling garden snails.

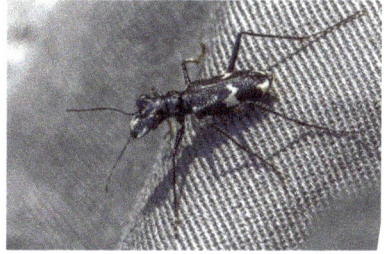

Some example of predators mentioned above

*A Carabid beetle (see opposite page) known as the Tree-trunk Tiger Beetle (**Distipsidera undulata**) mistaking a leg for its home. These beetles are voracious predators, as indicated by their prominent eyes and strong mandibles - this is not a beetle you want inside your trousers.*   Teale Britstra

*A Blue Tongue lizard making a meal of a Common Brown Garden Snail (**Helix aspersa**).*   Chris Schwencke

*A Tachinid fly, possibly a **Senostoma** sp. patrolling a plant in search of prey.*

Tachinid flies (see pages 76-80) are parasitoids of a diverse range of insects, spiders and snails.   Helen Schwencke

While many true bugs make their living by sucking sap from plants, predatory bugs, which are mentioned on pages 76 - 77 above, eat animals. Those mentioned are found in different Families of Hemiptera: Reduviidae (known as Assassin Bugs), Pentatomidae, Subfamily Asopinae (known as Predatory Stink Bugs) and Nabidae (known as Damsel Bugs). These creatures have adapted to using their rostrum, also known as a proboscis, to puncture the skin of other insects. The common predatory stink bugs of gardens are generalist predators of soft skinned insects, including many insect larvae. Assassin bugs feed on both soft-skinned insects, and also hard-skinned insects, such as beetles. Damsel Bugs feed on soft-skinned insects such as aphids.

*A 4th or 5th instar Common Assassin Bug probably **Pristhesancus plagipennis** making a meal of a Dainty Swallowtail caterpillar (**Papilio anactus**).*   Annette Dexter

*A Spined Predatory Shield Bug, probably **Oechalia schellenbergii**, feeding on a Glasswing butterfly larva (**Acraea andromacha**).*   Annette Dexter

7. Building ecological complexity

The pupa of an Ichneumon wasp (**Hyposoter didymator**). These parasitoid wasps were introduced in the 1980s to control Noctuid moth caterpillars. An unidentified Chalcid wasp is injecting its eggs into the pupa (notice its ovipositor at the end of its abdomen). The eggs will hatch into larvae which will devour the pupa from inside - a parasitoid of a parasitoid!
Ute Harder de Sohnrey

A female Diurnal Predatory Katydid, **Austrophlugis orumbera**, also known as a Swayer, for its side to side rocking motion when at rest. Many katydids are herbivores but some are predators or scavengers.
Helen Schwencke

An unidentified, nocturnal, predatory Mantispid, also called a Mantid Fly, or Mantis Lacewing. It was attracted to a UV-emitting light. Its forelegs are adapted to grab prey animals.
Helen Schwencke

With the complexity-enhancing and competition-reducing methods for gardening and producing food that are suggested in this book, parasitoids, such as small wasps, lacewings and flies, are mentioned repeatedly as a form of ecological control. These are only some of the vast diversity of different insect Orders that have members that are predators and which may also be able to play a bigger role in our gardens. Some species discussed are already frequently present in many gardens. For others to find their place, they will need a greater diversity of plants, and other conditions to be present, some of which are mentioned in the Wildlife friendly gardening section.

While some predators and parasitoids are already being used to control the competition for our food, others, such as robber flies, various predatory katydids, dragonflies and damselflies, which are present less frequently, could also be encouraged to hang out, and help out, in our gardens. The idea here is to learn to rely on a much higher diversity, even if some of these will be less frequent garden residents. It is through using strategies that can attract the widest possible diversity that this approach will help, whether the species are present in smaller or larger numbers.

While some of the species discussed are generalists that will parasitise a number of the species we are looking to control, they usually still utilise species within the same Family of insects. However, many are selective, that is, specialists, utilising one or a few closely related prey species as their food sources.

In some situations, there are parasitoids of the parasitoids, and even parasitoids of them - mostly tiny wasps laying their eggs in the larvae of slightly bigger wasps. These are then 2nd and 3rd level carnivores in the food web (see diagram p. 17).

Studies of a range of host plants have shown that when a herbivore eats a host plant, the plant produces chemicals to alert its sibling plants and also to alert the predators and parasitoids of that herbivore. The higher order predators or parasitoids of the first level predator or

parasitoid may also be alerted by the plant's defence chemicals and the insect herbivores, in turn, have their own strategies to evade their predators and parasitoids. The
relationships between these herbivores, their host plants and their predators and parasitoids can be amazingly complex.

In commercial cropping situations, farmers sometimes purchase specific parasitoids
and predatory insects to ensure that populations of herbivores do not explode and
utilise too much of their crops. These are also becoming available to gardeners. The bio-
control agents currently available for purchase are frequently generalists, which can be
effective but in a 'scatter gun' way that affects a range of herbivores indiscriminately.

Research is showing that if we enhance the biodiversity of native plants in a garden
or other managed ecosystem, we will provide habitat and food for a wider range of
specialist predators and parasitoids [35,36,37]. They, in turn, will attract their own higher
order predators and parasitoids, thus creating a more complex ecology that will act as
a check on any one herbivore getting 'out of control' in our gardens.

Ninety two percent of all named species are invertebrates, and yet we see so few of
them in our gardens. So where are they?

In this book we have illustrated mainly creatures that are diurnal, (active during the
day), but many are nocturnal, (active during the night). Some nocturnal species may
be active in our gardens but remain unnoticed, except for evidence of their night-time
activities, such as chewed leaves or the actions of predators such as the lifeless car-
casses of those night-feeding herbivores.

It is also difficult for us to support more native invertebrates in our gardens unless
we change the plant species we use for interplanting amongst our food plants. Including
local native plant species will support this greater diversity, particularly if we include
the specific plants that particular insects require. There is thus a great opportunity to
enhance biodiversity and expand ecological complexity considerably in our gardens,
which will also help raise awareness and understanding of gardening ecology and
ultimately help reverse the declines of both species and populations of invertebrates.

8. Native food recipes

The recipes in this section use ingredients from the *Native Food Plants We Can Share* section pp. 46 - 73. The next edition will contain more recipes. Let us know if you have any favourites that include any of the native foods mentioned in this book.

Macadamia, Warrigal Greens and Lemon Myrtle Pesto

(from Cherikoff, V. Uniquely Australian, Bush Tucker Supply, Sydney, 1992)

3 cups (200g) fresh leaves of warrigal greens (*Tetragonia tetragonioides*)
½ cup (50g) macadamia nuts
1 clove garlic
1 cup macadamia oil
1 tbsp ground dried lemon myrtle leaves (*Backhousia citriodora*)
½ teaspoon native pepper leaf (*Tasmannia insipida*) or black pepper
    salt to taste

Blanch warrigal green leaves in boiling water for 2 minutes. Drain, rinse with cold water, then squeeze water out of leaves with your hand.

Chop macadamia nuts, peel and crush garlic. Fry nuts and garlic lightly in 1 teaspoon of oil for 3 minutes.

Process nuts and garlic in a food processor, then add warrigal greens, oil and seasoning. Process until smooth.

Use straight away or store in a covered container in the fridge.

Bunya Dooja Cake

250g bunya nuts or 175g dried bunya grits (*Araucaria bidwillii*)
6   dooja limes (native round limes - *Citrus australis*)
6   eggs, beaten
250g sugar
1 tsp baking powder

Boil dooja limes in a little water in a covered saucepan for 20 minutes, turning regularly. Allow to cool then cut open, remove pips and chop roughly.

Boil bunya nuts for 20 minutes, then briefly process in a food processor to produce a coarse bunya mince. If using dried bunyas, cover bunya grits in boiling water, allow to soak for one hour, then drain off excess water.

Preheat the oven to 190°C and oil and flour a springform tin. Blend limes with remaining ingredients thoroughly in a food processor. Pour batter into prepared tin.

Bake for 1hour and 15 minutes. Cool in tin before turning out.

Serve with sour cream or yoghurt

9. Conclusion - What can we do?

Nature is in trouble, and that means we are too. Those creatures that make up the vast majority of animal species, the invertebrates, including especially insects, are suffering serious declines in numbers and diversity. We humans have cleared their habitat, changed the climate, displaced them with exotic species and poisoned them with pesticides.

These smaller and often ignored members of the web of life play key roles in converting plants into protein food for other animals, in decomposing dead organic material into soil-enriching nutrients and in pollinating flowering and fruiting plants.

In this light we can then start to re-think our approach to gardening. In particular, we can start to integrate a diverse range of native plants, including insect host plants and edible native or bushfood plants, with our exotic food plants. This one small step that will start a giant leap towards treating nature as an ally is the key to becoming "bug-friendly" or, more specifically, "beneficial insect friendly" gardeners. Though we need to remember that the "beneficial insects", our allies, need those that are our competitors, frequently called "pests", for their own survival.

As we grow in our understanding about how we need to respect nature and bring it back into our lives and into our local spaces and places, we will realise that other creatures will always want to share the food we produce. But if we accept this fact and build our gardens as complex ecosystems that include many and varied native plants, we can provide for both them and us. While this is harder to achieve in large scale agriculture, it is something we can start to understand and practice in our gardens.

As gardeners, we can lead by example and start spreading the word as far and wide as possible about what we are doing and why. If we build a critical mass of gardeners who are demonstrating the benefits of inviting nature to dinner by bringing biodiversity to our backyards, we can start to influence other land holders and start a much needed revolution in how we grow our food and manage our land in Australia and elsewhere.

We can start by simply indulging in the fun and pleasure of noticing and observing insects and other invertebrates in our gardens and local places. As you learn to notice these small creatures and their interactions with plants, we hope you will agree with, and spread, Helen's favourite expression -

"The only good leaf is a chewed leaf".

Your feedback please

As outlined in the "How to Use this Book" in the preliminary pages, this book is the first step of exploring how to increase biodiversity in our local spaces and places while also feeding ourselves. We are offering our first efforts at doing this here, hence calling it a preview edition.

We welcome any feedback you would like to share with us. Below are some prompts to help you give that feedback:

- Are there other issues that you think we should describe that are relevant to the aims of this book?

- Is there other relevant material that you think we should present?

- Are there areas that you would like more details about?

- Are there any mistakes or statements that you think are wrong?

- Is there anything that stands out for you?

- How practical are our suggestions and recommendations?

- Are there any other thoughts you would like to share with us?

And, if you are someone with specialised knowledge about specific plant-herbivore-carnivore and higher trophic level interactions between specific species and/or groups of species, we will welcome your input to the next iteration of this book.

Please send your feedback to info@earthling.com.au. Other options for how to share your feedback, other than emailing us, are outlined in "How to use this book", in the preliminary pages.

Next edition

Our intention is to release the first edition within 12 months of the release of this preview edition.

If you have purchased a Preview copy without contact with either of us as the authors, and you would like to obtain the full version, once released, at a discounted price please use one of the means of contacting us as per the "How to use this book section" see preliminary pages, and let us know.

Appendices

Appendix 1:

Site Assessment and Analysis

This appendix provides information on the 'layers' of site assessment and how to obtain the information you need to complete an analysis of your site before you start planting. It includes links to online tools and databases, most of which are specific to south east Queensland, but similar tools are available in other areas of Australia.

Appendix 2:

Some plants (mostly Edible) that pupport butterflies and other wildlife in south east Queensland and northern NSW

This appendix provides information on about 100 plants that are native to the Macleay-McPherson Overlap bioregion of south east Queensland and northern New South Wales, and which are food plants for the larvae or adults of local native butterflies, moths and other invertebrates. The list is still in development. Most of the plants are also edible 'bushfoods'.

The plants are grouped according to their size, form and sun/shade preference to help you decide which ones will be suitable for your garden and where to plant them. It is important to consider plants in this list against the assessment you make based in part on the regional ecosystem your property is located in, as per your site assessment (Appendix 1).

Appendix 3:

Where to obtain native and bushfood plants in SEQ & N NSW

This appendix provides the names, locations, websites and contact details of the many small community and commercial nurseries that sell local native plants, bushfood plants and some exotic fruit trees in south east Queensland and northern New South Wales.

This list is by no means complete. Please let us know about other local native plant nurseries.

Appendix 1

Site Assessment and Analysis

Landform and Regional Ecosystem	*Information Sources in South East Queensland*
Regional Ecosystem maps	https://apps.des.qld.gov.au/map-request/re-broad-veg-group/
Geology	https://www.qld.gov.au/environment/plants-animals/plants/ecosystems/descriptions/land-zones
Native vegetation	https://apps.des.qld.gov.au/regional-ecosystems/
Morphology and slopes	Observation and measurement Contour maps: http://qtopo.dnrm.qld.gov.au/mobile/, https://www.data.qld.gov.au/dataset/contours-5-metre-queensland-series

Climate

Climatic Zone – e.g. humid subtropics	
Precipitation, wind, temperature, seasonal change Frost	http://www.bom.gov.au/qld/ Observation Neighbours
Extremes – flood, drought, fire, cyclones	http://www.bom.gov.au/qld/ Neighbours
Predicted future climate change	https://www.climatechangeinaustralia.gov.au/en/climate-projections/

Water

Sources – roof, river, dams, mains, etc.	Observation
Flows – run-off patterns, concentration and dispersal areas	Observation, especially. during and after rain
Problems – boggy areas, flooding, dry spots etc.	Observation
Pollution	Observation, laboratory testing

Legal Issues

History of site uses, potential contamination and any resulting restrictions	Previous owner, neighbours https://www.qld.gov.au/environment/pollution/ management/contaminated-land/registers
Land use zoning and regulations Covenants, setbacks, easements, body corporation rules, etc.	http://cityplan2014maps.brisbane.qld.gov.au/ CityPlan/ Body corporate, landlord
Plant and weed regulations	https://www.daf.qld.gov.au/__data/assets/pdf_file/ 0004/383818/IPA-Restricted-plants-of-Qld.pdf https://weeds.brisbane.qld.gov.au/environmental-weeds

Infrastructure, Access and Circulation

Buildings, sheds, fences, dams, drains, swales, etc	Observation and measurement http://cityplan2014maps.brisbane.qld.gov.au/CityPlan/ https://www.google.com.au/maps/
Water, sewerage, storm water, power and telecom lines Septic leach fields	Dial B4 You Dig: https://www.1100.com.au/qld/about/ Observation
Activity nodes and existing zones of use	Interview, Observation
Flows of people, vehicles and materials, internal roads, paths etc.	Interview, Observation

Vegetation and Wildlife

Existing plant species – incl. niche analysis	Observation, knowledgeable friends, consultants Plant ID reference books: *Mountains to Mangroves, Wild Plants of Greater Brisbane, Rainforest Trees and Shrubs* Weed websites above Fb group: QLD Plant Identification
Architecture – layers, density, patterns, etc.	Observation
Wildlife species and habitat, food, water and shelter, incl. 'pest' species	Observation, knowledgeable friends, consultants Reference books: *Plant Pests, Diseases and Beneficials,* Fb group: Insect identification Australia

Microclimate

Define specific spaces	Observation
Seasonal patterns of sun/ shade, wind, soil moisture and frost	Observation, measurement
Slope aspect	Observation, measurement

Soil

Soil types: texture, structure, consistency, profile, drainage	DIY qualitative soil testing
Fertility: pH, % organic matter, soil organisms, nutrients (N, P, K, Ca, etc)	DIY pH test Quantitative soil test from a laboratory
Disturbance and erosion	Observation
Toxins (heavy metals, asbestos, pesticides, hydrocarbons, etc.)	Quantitative soil test from a laboratory

Aesthetics

Views, view lines, entries, outdoor 'rooms'	Observation
Sense of place, feng shui	Observation
Blighted areas, noise	Observation

Appendix 2

Some plants (mostly edible) that support butterflies and other wildlife in south east Queensland and northern NSW

Names	Character-istics, needs and functions	Edible parts	Butterflies and other wildlife supported

Understorey Trees and Shrubs - Moist Forest

Names	Characteristics, needs and functions	Edible parts	Butterflies and other wildlife supported
Alectryon *A. tomentosus,* *A. subcinereus,* *A. coriaceous,* *A. connatus*		Fruit - small	Large Purple Line-blue (*Nacaduba berenice*) Hairy Line-blue (*Erysichton lineata*) Short-tailed Line-blue (*Prosotas felderi*) Glistening Blue (*Sahulana scintallata*) Pencilled Blues (*Candalides* spp.) These feed on the flowers and very new shoots
Aniseed Myrtle *Syzygium anisata*		Leaves for spice, tea	Nectar feeding insects
Aspens *Acronychia oblongifolia,* *A. acidula,* *A. wilcoxiana,* *A. pubescens*		Fruit - tart citrus flavour in sauces	Gelechiid moth (*Dichomeris capnites*) Tineoid moth (*Acrocercops macaria*)
Climbing Senna *Senna gaudichaudii*	Nitrogen fixer. A scrambler that can be pruned into a shrub		Yellow Migrant (*Catopsilia gorgophone*) Orange Migrant (*Catopsilia scylla*) Small Grass-yellow (*Eurema smilax*) Large Grass-yellow (*Eurema hecabe*) Pale Ciliate-blue (*Anthene lycaenoides*) Blue-banded and other buzz-pollinator bees (*Amegilla* spp.)
Bolwarra *Eupomatia laurina*	Needs rainforest weevils (*Elleschodes* spp.) for pollination	Fruit	Eastern Dusk-flat (*Chaetocneme beata*)
Brush Senna *Senna acclinis*	Nitrogen fixer. Listed as Near Threatened		Yellow Migrant (*Catopsilia gorgophone*) Small Grass-yellow (*Eurema smilax*) Large Grass-yellow (*Eurema hecabe*)
Caper bushes *Capparis arborea* *C. velutina*		Fruit	Caper White (*Belenois java*) Caper Gull (*Cepora perimale*) Striated Pearl-white (*Elodina parthia*)
Cluster Berry *Micromelum minutum*		Fruit	Southern Pearl-white (*Elodina angulipennis*) Orchard Swallowtail (*Papilio aegeus*) Fuscous Swallowtail (*Papilio fuscus*) Nectar feeding insects

Names cont.	Character-istics, needs and functions	Edible parts	Butterflies and other wildlife supported
Coffee bush *Breynia oblongifolia*	Hardy, also grows from root suckers	Fruit - eat when black (only a few)	Large Grass-yellow (*Eurema hecabe*) Noctuid moths (*Parallelia* spp.) Tineoid moth (*Phyllocnistis diaugella*) Gracillariid moths (*Epicphala* spp.) Green Jewel bug (*Lampromicra senator*)
Corduroy Tamarind *Mischarytera lautereriana*		Fruit	Hairy Line-blue (*Erysichton lineata*)
Lemon Myrtle *Backhousia citriodora*		Leaves for spice, tea	Nectar feeding insects
Lime Berry *Glycosmis trifoliata*		Fruit - tangy citrus flavour	Orchard Swallowtail (*Papilio aegeus*) Fuscous Swallowtail (*Papilio fuscus*)
Orange Thorn *Pittosporum multiflorum*	Moist areas only	Fruit	Bright Copper (*Paralucia aurifer*) - needs ants (*Anonychomyrma* sp.)
Sandpaper Figs *Ficus coronata F. opposita*	Fruits best in moist soil	Fruit - sweet and juicy if grown in moist soil	Purple Moonbeam (*Philiris innotatus*) Common Crow (*Euploea core*) Chalcidoid Fig Wasps
Silky Myrtle *Decaspermum humile*		Fruit, leaves for tea	Nectar feeding insects

Understorey Trees and Shrubs - Dry Forest

Cinnamon myrtle *Backhousia myrtifolia*		Leaves for spice, tea	Nectar feeding insects Tessellated Stick-insect (*Anchiale austrotessulata*)
Coastal Banksia *Banksia integrifolia*		Nectar, seeds	Double-headed hawk moth (*Coequosa triangularis*)
Currant bush *Carissa ovata*		Fruit	Common Crow (*Euploea core*) (rarely) Hairy Line-blue (*Erysichton lineata*)
Koda *Ehretia accuminata*		Fruit - small	White-banded Plane (*Phaedyma shepherdi*) Fruit eating birds
Native Cherry *Exocarpus cupressiformis*	Partly parasitic on roots of other plants e.g. Eucalypts	Fruit - small, sweet	Spotted Jezebel (*Delias aganippe*) Fiery Jewel (*Hypochrysops ignitus*) - needs ants (*Papyrius* spp.) *Gendura punctigera* (moth) *Acyphas leucomelas* (moth)
Native Indigo *Indigofera australis*	Nitrogen fixer		Tailed Pea-blue (*Lampides boeticus*) Common Grass-blue (*Zizina labradus*)

Names	Characteristics, needs and functions	Edible parts	Butterflies and other wildlife supported

Sun-loving Small Trees and Shrubs

Names	Characteristics, needs and functions	Edible parts	Butterflies and other wildlife supported
Blue Tongue *Melastoma affine*	Prefers moist soil	Fruit	Coral Jewel (*Hypochrysops miskini*) - needs attendant ants (*Anonychomyrma gilberti*)
Brisbane Wattle *Acacia fimbriata*	Nitrogen fixer Rapid growing but short-lived		Imperial Hairstreak (*Jalmenus evagoras*) - needs attendant ants (*Iridomyrmex* spp.
Dooja Lime *Citrus australis*		Fruit for jams, cakes	Orchard Swallowtail (*Papilio aegeus*) Dainty Swallowtail (*Papilio anactus*)
Finger Lime *Citrus australasica*	Plants grafted onto exotic citrus rootstock produce fruit earlier and more abundantly	Fruit for jams, drinks, garnish See recipe	Orchard Swallowtail (*Papilio aegeus*) Dainty Swallowtail (*Papilio anactus*) Fuscous Swallowtail (*Papilio fuscus*) Small birds e.g. Double-barred Finch (*Poephila bichenovii*)
Hickory Wattles *Acacia disparrima* *A. aulocarpa*	Nitrogen fixers Rapid growing but short-lived		Fiery Jewel (*Hypochrysops ignitus*) - needs ants (*Papyrius* spp.) Moonlight Jewel (*Hypochrysops delicia*) - needs Crematogaster ants Double-spotted Line-blue (*Nacaduba biocellata*) Short-tailed Line-blue (*Prosotas felderi*) Small Purple Line-blue (*Prosotas dubiosa*) Glistening Blue (*Sahulana scintillata*) Wattle Blue (*Theclinesthes miskini*)
Midyimberry *Austromyrtus dulcis*	Prefers sandy coastal soils	Fruit	Nectar-feeding butterflies
Native Mulberry *Pipturus argenteus*	Fast growing. Tolerates regular cutting back	Small snacking fruit	Jezebel Nymph (*Mynes geoffroyi*) Speckled Line-blue (*Catopyrops florinda*) Lacewings, Grasshoppers, Beetles, Small spiders, Fruit-eating birds
Old-man Saltbush *Atriplex nummularia*	Drought tolerant	Leaves - boiled	Saltbush Blue (*Theclinesthes serpentata*) Stingless bees
Peanut Tree *Sterculia quadrifida*	Semi-deciduous in spring	Seeds	Chrome Awl (*Hasora chromus*)
Blackthorn *Bursaria spinosa*			Nectar feeding insects

Names	Characteristics, needs and functions	Edible parts	Butterflies and other wildlife supported

Large Trees

Names	Characteristics, needs and functions	Edible parts	Butterflies and other wildlife supported
Black Wattle *Acacia concurrens* *A. leiocalyx*	Nitrogen fixers		Moonlight Jewel (*Hypochrysops delicia*) - needs *Crematogaster* ants Emerald Hairstreak (*Jalmenus daemeli*) - needs *Iridomyrmex* spp. Ants Imperial Hairstreak (*J. evagoras*) - needs *Iridomyrmex* spp. ants Stencilled Hairstreak (*J. ictinus*) - usually needs *Iridomyrmex purpureus* ants Two-spotted Line-blue (*Nacaduba biocellata*) Short-tailed Line-blue (*Prosotas felderi*) Purple Line-blue (*P. dubiosa*) Glistening Blue (*Sahulana scintillata*)
Cabbage-tree Palm *Livistona australis*		Apical bud or 'heart'	Orange Palm Dart (*Cephrenes augiades*)
Flame tree Lacebark Kurrajong *Brachychiton acerifolium* *B. discolor* *B. populneus*		Seeds - need to rub off irritant yellow coating. Like sunflower seeds	Tailed Emperor (*Polyura sempronius*) White-banded Plane (*Phaedyma shepherdi*) Common Pencilled-blue (*Candalides absimilis*)
Green Wattle *Acacia irrorata*	Nitrogen fixer		Tailed Emperor (*Polyura sempronius*) Large Grass-yellow (*Eurema hecabe*) Two-spotted Line-blue (*Nacaduba biocellata*) Moonlight Jewel (*Hypochrysops delicia*) - needs *Crematogaster* spp. ants Emerald Hairstreak (*Jalmenus daemeli*) - needs *Iridomyrmex* spp. ants Imperial Hairstreak (*J. evagoras*) - needs *Iridomyrmex* spp.ants Stencilled Hairstreak (*J. ictinus*) - usually needs *Iridomyrmex purpureus* ants
Macadamia *Macadamia integrifolia* *M. tetraphylla*	Susceptible to wind damage	Nuts See recipe	Bright Cornelian (*Deuodorix diovis*) Common Pencilled-blue (*Candalides absimilis*) Short-tailed Line-blue (*Prosotas felderi*) Large Purple Line-blue (*Nacaduba berenice*) Purple Line-blue (*P. dubiosa*) A cup moth (*Anaxidia lozogramma*) Double-headed Hawk moth (*Coequosia triangularis*) Macadmia leaf-miner moth (*Acrocercops chionosema*)

Names	Character-istics, needs and functions	Edible parts	Butterflies and other wildlife supported
Native Tamarind *Diploglottis australis*		Fruit - sour, makes good sauces, jams, drinks.	Bright Cornelian (*Deuodorix diovis*)
Shiny-leaved Stinging tree *Dendrocnide photinophylla*	Leaves, fruit have stinging hairs	Fruit Beware of stinging hairs	Jezebel Nymph (*Mynes geoffroyi*)

Groundcovers and Herbaceous Perennials

Names	Character-istics, needs and functions	Edible parts	Butterflies and other wildlife supported
Arrowhead Violet *Viola betonicifolia*	Needs moisture and partial shade	Flowers	Laced Fritillary (*Argyreus hyperbius*) - Endangered
Emu Foot *Cullen tenax*	Nitrogen fixer	Seed	Chequered Swallowtail (*Papilio demoleus*) Common Grass-blue (*Zizina labradus*) Tailed Pea-blue (*Lampides boeticus*)
Hairy Tick Trefoil *Desmodium heterocarpon*	Nitrogen fixer		Common Grass-blue (*Zizina labradus*) Orange-tipped Pea-blue (*Everes lacturnus*)
Native Plumbago *Plumbago zeylanica*			Plumbago Blue (*Leptopes plinius*)
Native sarsparilla *Hardenbergia violaceae*	Nitrogen fixer	Leaves for tea	
Pigface *Carpobrotus glaucescens*	Tolerates salty environ-ment	Fruit	Nectar feeding insects
Shade Plantain *Plantago debilis*		Leaves & seeds	Meadow Argus (*Junonia villida*)
Ruby Saltbush *Enchylaema tomentosa*	Drought and salt tolerant	Fruit	Samphire Blue (*Theclinesthes sulpitius*)
Samphire *Sarcocornia quinqueflora*	Needs light, well-drained salty soil	Stems - boiled or steamed	Samphire Blue (*Theclinesthes sulpitius*)
Sea Blite *Sueda australis*	Needs light, well-drained salty soil	Stems - boiled or steamed	Samphire Blue (*Theclinesthes sulpitius*)
Stinging Nettle *Urtica incisa*	Stinging hairs on leaves	Leaves - boiled, or thoroughly wilted	Yellow Admiral (*Vanessa itea*)

Names	Character-istics, needs and functions	Edible parts	Butterflies and other wildlife supported

Vines

Names	Character-istics, needs and functions	Edible parts	Butterflies and other wildlife supported
Bush Caper *Capparis lasianthus*	Vine or small shrub Drought tolerant	Fruit	Caper Gull (*Cepora perimale*) Caper White (*Belenois java*) Southern Pearl-white (*Elodina angulipennis*) Striated Pearl-white (*Elodina parthia*)
Climbing Caper *Capparis sarmentosa*	Needs moisture	Fruit	Caper Gull (*Cepora perimale*) Caper White (*Belenois java*) Striated Pearl-white (*Elodina parthia*)
Cockspur *Maclura cochinensis*	Very prickly	Fruit - tasty	Small birds
Millaa Millaa *Eleagnus triflora*		Fruit - tasty	Indigo Flash (*Rapala varuna*)
Monkey-rope *Parsonsia straminea*	Vigorous, hardy		Common Crow (*Euploea core*)
Native Grape *Clematocissus opaca*	Needs moisture, partial shade	Fruit	Joseph's Coat Moth (*Agarista agricola*) Crow Moth (*Cruria donowani*)
Native or Blunt-leaved Passionvine *Passiflora aurantia*		Fruit	Glasswing (*Achrea andromacha*)
Pencil Yam *Dioscorea transversa*		Pencil sized tuber (boiled or baked)	Yam Hawk Moth (*Theretra nessus*) Cacao Armyworm (*Tiracola plagiata*)
Scarlet Coral-pea *Kennedia rubicunda*	Nitrogen fixer, attractive red flowers	Leaves for tea	Tailed Pea-blue (*Lampides boeticus*)
Slender Grape *Cayratia clematidea*	Needs moisture, partial shade	Fruit	Joseph's Coat Moth (*Agarista agricola*) Crow Moth (*Cruria donowani*)
Zig-zag Vine *Melodorum leichhardtii*		Fruit - tasty	Pale Green Triangle (*Graphium eurypylus*) Four-barred Swordtail (*Protographium leosthenes*) Eastern Dusk-flat (*Chaetocneme beata*)

Names	Character- istics, needs and functions	Edible parts	Butterflies and other wildlife supported

Grasses, Sedges and Rushes

Names	Character- istics, needs and functions	Edible parts	Butterflies and other wildlife supported
Barb-wire Grass *Cymbopogon refractus*		Leaves for tea	No-brand Grass-dart (*Taractrocera ina*) Evening Brown (*Melanitis leda*)
Blady Grass *Imperata cylindrica*	Hardy, can be invasive	Shoots, inflorescence and roots	Evening Brown (*Melanitis leda*) Dusky Knight (*Ypthima arctous*) Greenish Darter (*Telicota ancilla*) White-banded Grass-dart (*Taractrocera papyria*) Dark Grass-dart (*Suniana lascivia*)
Basket grass Creeping Beard Grass *Oplismenus aemulus O. undulatus*	Good ground cover		Orange Bush-brown (*Mycalesis terminus*) Wonder Brown (*Heteronympha mirifica*) Lilac Grass-skipper (*Toxidia doubledayi*) White-brand Grass-skipper (*T. reitmanni*) Orange Grass-dart (*Oxybadistes ardea*)
Graceful grass *Ottochloa gracillima*	Cool, moist area		Brown Ringlet (*Hypocysta metirius*) Wonder Brown (*Heteronympha mirifica*) Lilac Grass-skipper (*Toxidia doubledayi*) White-brand Grass-skipper (*T. reitmanni*)
Kangaroo grass *Themeda triandra*	Partial shade, drought tolerant	Seeds ground for flour	Evening Brown (*Melanitis leda*) Common Brown (*Heteronympha merope*) Shouldered Brown (*H. penelope*) Ringed Xenica (*Geitoneura acantha*) Marbled Xenica (G. klugii) Grey Ringlet (*Hypocysta pseudirius*) Orange Ringlet (*H. adiante*)
Mat rushes *Lomandra longifolia, L.hystrix, L. multiflora, L.filiformis, L.confertifolia*	Hardy	Flowers in drinks, Leaf bases to chew	Many species of Skipper butterflies (*Trapezites* spp.)
Saw sedges Gahnia spp		Seeds ground for flour	Sword-grass Brown (*Tisiphone abeona*) Many species of Sedge Skippers (*Hesperilla* spp.)
Tussock grasses *Poa labillardieri, P. queenslandica P. sieberiana, P. tenera*	Cool, moist area		Banks' Brown (*Heteronympha banksii*) Common Brown (*H. merope*) Spotted Brown (*H. paradelpha*) Ringed Xenica (*Geitoneura acantha*) Marbled Xenica (*G. klugii*) Barred Skipper (*Dispar compacta*) Bright Shield-skipper (*Signeta flammeata*) Chequered Grass-skipper (*Anisynta tillyardi*) Banded Grass-skipper (*Toxidia parvula*) Southern Grass-skipper (*T. andersoni*) White Grass-dart (*Taractrocera papyria*)

Appendix 3

Where to obtain native and bushfood plants in SEQ & N NSW

B4C Native Plant Nursery
Cnr Wright St & 1358 Old Cleveland
Rd, Carindale QLD 4152
Ph: 07 3398 8003
e: b4c@bulimbacreek.org.au
I: https://bulimbacreek.org.au/nursery/

Barung Community Native Plant Nursery
Porters Lane, North Maleny QLD 4552
M: / ph: 0429 943 152, 07 5302 9900
e: nursery@barunglandcare.org.au
I: http://www.barunglandcare.org.au/

Burringbar Rainforest Nursery
380 Burringbar Road, Upper Burringbar
NSW 2483
Ph: 02 6677 1088
e: brnursery1@gmail.com
I: https://burringbarrainforestnursery.com.au/

Daley's Fruit Tree Nursery
36 Daley's Lane, Geneva via Kyogle
NSW 2474
e: order@daleysfruit.com.au
I: https://www.daleysfruit.com.au/
Stocks Exotic Fruit Trees as well

Northey Street City Farm,
16 Victoria St, Windsor QLD 4030
Ph: 07 3857 8775
e: nursery@nscf.org.au
I: https://www.nscf.org.au
Stocks Exotic Fruit Trees as well

Fairhill Native Plants
114-132 Farhill Rd, Ninderry QLD 4561
M: 0410 585 742
e: retail@fairhill.com.au
I: https://www.fairhill.com.au/

Forest Heart Eco Nursery
20 Coral St, Maleny QLD 4552
Ph: 07 5435 2193
e: nursery@foresthart.com.au
I: https://www.foresthart.com.au/

Indigiscapes
17 Runnymede Road, Capalaba, QLD 4157
Ph: 07 3820 1119
e: indigiscapes@redland.qld.gov.au
I: https://indigiscapes.redland.qld.gov.au/
info/5/nursery

Kumbartcho
15 Bunya Pine Ct, Eatons Hill QLD 4037
Ph: 07 3264 3953
e: info@kumbartcho.org.au
I: https://www.kumbartcho.org.au/nursery

Michelle's Native Plants
Various markets Gold Coast QLD
e: michellesnativeplants@bigpond.com
Facebook: I: https://www.facebook.com/
Michelles-Native-Plants-1275066389218960

Nielsen's Native Nursery
49-51 Beenleigh-Redland Bay Rd,
Loganholme QLD 4129
Ph: 07 3806 1414
I: https://nielsensnativenursery.com.au
Stocks Exotic Fruit Trees as well

Paten Park Native Nursery
57 Paten Rd, The Gap QLD 4061
Ph: 07 3300 6304
I: https://ppnn.org.au

Pete's Hobby Nursery
10 Patrick St Lowood QLD 4311
M: 0412 243 740
e: peteshobbynursery@iprimus.com.au
I: https://www.peteshobbynursery.com.au/

Save our Waterways Now
57 Paten Rd, The Gap QLD 4061
M: 0423 763 361
e: info@saveourwaterwaysnow.com.au
I: www.saveourwaterwaysnow.com.au

Tallegalla Fruit Trees
19 Cochranes Rd, Tallegalla, QLD 4340
Ph: (07) 54644032
e: sales@tallegallafruittrees.com.au
I: https://www.tallegallafruittrees.com.au/
Stocks mostly exotics, with some natives

Wallum Nursery
1237 New Cleveland Rd, Gumdale, QLD 4154
Ph: 07 3823 3233
e: info@wallumnurseries.com
I: http://www.wallumnurseries.com/

Witjuti Grub Bushfood Nursery
84 Falls Creek Road, Obi Obi QLD 4574
M: / ph: 07 5446 9265
I: www.witjutigrub.com.au

11. References

1. Conrad, K. F., Warren, M. S., Fox, R., Parsons, M. S. & Woiwod, I. P. Rapid declines of common, widespread British moths provide evidence of an insect biodiversity crisis. *Biological Conservation* vol. 132 279–291 (2006).

2. The Selangor Declaration: Conservation of Fireflies | Lampyrid Volume 3 2014. http://www.firefliesandglow-worms.co.uk/lampyrid-journal/vol2/ selangor-declaration-conservation-of-fireflies.html.

3. Sánchez-Bayo, F. & Wyckhuys, K. A. G. Worldwide decline of the entomofauna: A review of its drivers. *Biological Conservation* vol. 232 8–27 (2019).

4. Dirzo, R. et al. Defaunation in the Anthropocene. *Science* vol. 345 401–406 (2014).

5. Seibold, S. et al. Arthropod decline in grasslands and forests is associated with landscape-level drivers. *Nature* vol. 574 671–674 (2019).

6. Lister, B. C. & Garcia, A. Climate-driven declines in arthropod abundance restructure a rainforest food web. *Proceedings of the National Academy of Sciences* vol. 115 E10397–E10406 (2018).

7. Western Monarch Butterflies Continue to Decline | Xerces Society. https:// xerces.org/press/western-monarch-butterflies-continue-to-decline.

8. Bad news for Europe's bumblebees. IUCN https://www.iucn.org/content/bad-news-europes-bumblebees (2014).

9. Cameron, S. A. et al. Patterns of widespread decline in North American bumble bees. *Proc. Natl. Acad. Sci. U. S. A.* 108, 662–667 (2011).

10. The IUCN Red List of Threatened Species. *IUCN Red List of Threatened Species* https://www.iucnredlist.org/en.

11. Binetti, R., Costamagna, F. M. & Marcello, I. Exponential growth of new chemicals and evolution of information relevant to risk control. *Ann. Ist. Super. Sanita* 44, 13–15 (2008).

12. Tallamy, D. W. *Bringing Nature Home: How You Can Sustain Wildlife with Native Plants,* Updated and Expanded. (Timber Press, 2009).

13. File:Tree of Living Organisms 2.png - Wikimedia Commons. https:// commons.wikimedia.org/wiki/File:Tree_of_Living_Organisms_2.png.

14. Wheeler, Q. D. Insect Diversity and Cladistic Constraints. *Annals of the Entomological Society of America* vol. 83 1031–1047 (1990), cited by Penick, C. & Sorger, M. Updating the Species Scape http://yourwildlife.org/2016/09/ updating-the-species-scape/ (2016)

15. Website. *IUCN Red List version 2020-1: Table 1a* https://www.iucnredlist.org/ resources/summary-statistics. (2020)

16. Gering, J. C., DeRennaux, K. A. & Crist, T. O. Scale dependence of effective specialization: its analysis and implications for estimates of global insect species richness. *Diversity and Distributions* vol. 13 115–125 (2007).

17. Foottit, R. G. & Adler, P. H. *Insect Biodiversity: Science and Society*. (John Wiley & Sons, 2017).

18. Becerra, J. X. On the factors that promote the diversity of herbivorous insects and plants in tropical forests. *Proc. Natl. Acad. Sci. U. S. A.* 112, 6098–6103 (2015).

19. Singer, M. C., Thomas, C. D. & Parmesan, C. Rapid human-induced evolution of insect–host associations. *Nature* vol. 366 681–683 (1993).

20. Braschler, B. & Hill, J. K. Role of larval host plants in the climate-driven range expansion of the butterfly Polygonia c-album. *J. Anim. Ecol.* 76, 415–423 (2007).

21. Maoela, M. A., Roets, F., Jacobs, S. M. & Esler, K. J. Restoration of invaded Cape Floristic Region riparian systems leads to a recovery in foliage-active arthropod alpha- and beta-diversity. *Journal of Insect Conservation* vol. 20 85–97 (2016).

22. Heleno, R. H., Ceia, R. S., Ramos, J. A. & Memmott, J. Effects of alien plants on insect abundance and biomass: a food-web approach. *Conserv. Biol.* 23, 410–419 (2009).

23. Meijer, K., Schilthuizen, M., Beukeboom, L. & Smit, C. A review and meta-analysis of the enemy release hypothesis in plant–herbivorous insect systems. *PeerJ* vol. 4 e2778 (2016).

24. Sinclair, R. J. & Hughes, L. Leaf miners: the hidden herbivores. *Austral Ecol.* 35, 300–313 (2010).

25. Thabet, A. A., Youssef, F. S., El-Shazly, M. & Singab, A. N. B. Sterculia and Brachychiton: a comprehensive overview on their ethnopharmacology, biological activities, phytochemistry and the role of their gummy exudates in drug delivery. *J. Pharm. Pharmacol.* 70, 450–474 (2018).

26. Website. Understanding Helicoverpa ecology and biology in southern Queensland https://www.daf.qld.gov.au/__data/assets/pdf_file/0005/72689/Insects-Helicoverpa-ecology-biology.pdf.

27. Website. Corn earworm and native budworm https://www.daf.qld.gov.au/business-priorities/agriculture/plants/fruit-vegetable/insect-pests/corn-earworm-native-budworm.

28. Website. Fruit piercing moth https://www.daf.qld.gov.au/business-priorities/agriculture/plants/fruit-vegetable/insect-pests/fruit-piercing-moth.

29. Website. Macadamia nutborer. https://www.daf.qld.gov.au/business-priorities/agriculture/plants/fruit-vegetable/insect-pests/macadamia-nutborer (2018).

30. Website: Whiteflies – Bugs For Bugs. https://bugsforbugs.com.au/whats-your-pest/whiteflies/.

31. Website. Biological control of grapevine scales, Department of Primary Industries, Victoria 30 June, 2008. https://www.wineaustralia.com/getmedia/ce1f3d98-214e-4195-b6ca-5f7c80dc4f38/DNR03-01, p. 29

32. Website. Fruitspotting bugs 2016 www.dpi.nsw.gov.au NSW DPI MANAGEMENT GUIDE.

33. Michaels, F. & Fitzsimmons, N. Fruitspotting Bug Organic Control Information. http://greenharvest.com.au/PestControlOrganic/Information/FruitspottingBugControl.html.

34. Michaels, F. & Fitzsimmons, N. Grasshopper Organic Control Information. https://greenharvest.com.au/PestControlOrganic/Information/GrasshopperControl.html.

35. Tscharntke, T., Klein, A. M., Kruess, A., Steffan-Dewenter, I. & Thies, C. Landscape perspectives on agricultural intensification and biodiversity and ecosystem service management. Ecology Letters vol. 8 857–874 (2005).

36. Isaacs, R., Tuell, J., Fiedler, A., Gardiner, M. & Landis, D. Maximizing arthropod-mediated ecosystem services in agricultural landscapes: the role of native plants. *Frontiers in Ecology and the Environment* vol. 7 196–203 (2009).

37. Snyder, W. E. Give predators a complement: Conserving natural enemy biodiversity to improve biocontrol. *Biological Control* vol. 135 73–82 (2019).

38. van Klink, R. et al. Meta-analysis reveals declines in terrestrial but increases in freshwater insect abundances. *Science* 368, 417- 420 (2020).

39. Hallmann, C., Sorg, M., Jongejans, E.,Siepel, H., Hofland, N., Schwan, H., Stenmans, W., Müller, A., Sumser, H., Hörren, T., Goulson, D., de Kroon, H. More than 75 percent decline over 27 years in total flying insect biomass in protected areas. *PLoS ONE*, 12 (10): e0185809 (2017)

40. *Terrestrial Invertebrate Status Review: Brisbane City,* p.30. (Queensland Museum, 2006)

41. Blakemore R.J., Paoletti, M. Australian Earthworms as a Natural Agroecological Resource. *Annals of Arid Zone* 45(3&4): 1-22 (2006)

An extra thought:

As the American comedian George Carlin once said,
the caterpillar does all the work, but the butterfly gets all the publicity!

12. Bibliography and Further Reading

Books

Braby, M.F. *Butterflies of Australia.* (CSIRO Melbourne, 2004)

Common, I.F.B. *Moths of Australia.* (Melbourne University Press, Melbourne, 1990)

Cribb, A.B., Cribb, J.W. *Wild Food in Australia.* (William Collins, Sydney, 1986)

Finney, V. *Transformations: Harriett and Helena Scott - colonial Sydney's finest natural history painters.* (New South Publishing, Sydney, 2018)

Footit, R. G., Adler, P. H. (editors). *Insect Biodiversity : Science and Society, Volume 1.* 2nd ed. (John Wiley & Sons, Incorporated, 2017). Digital edition available via Queensland State Library - ProQuest Ebook Central, http://ebookcentral.proquest.com/lib/slq/detail.action?docID=4923293.

Gleeson, M. *Miniature Lives: Identifying Insects in Your Home and Garden.* (CSIRO Publishing, 2016)

Harden, G., McDonald, W. J. F., Williams, J. *Rainforest Trees and Shrubs: A Field Guide to their Identification.* (Gwen Harding Publishing, 2006)

Hockings, F.D. Pests, *Diseases and Beneficials: Friends and Foes of Australian Gardens.* (CSIRO Publishing, 2014)

Jordan, F., Schwencke, H. *Create More Butterflies.* (Brisbane, Earthling Enterprises, 2005)

Leiper, G. *Mutooroo: Plant Use by Australian Aboriginal People.* (Assembly Kingswood Press, Brisbane, 1984)

Leiper, G. et al. *Mangroves to Mountains: A Field Guide to the Plants of South East Queensland* (SGAP Logan River Branch, 2012)

Low, T. *Wild Food Plants of Australia.* (Angus and Robertson, Sydney, 1984)

Marshall, T. Bug: *The Ultimate Gardener's Guide to Organic Pest Control.* (ABC Books, 2010)

Moss, J. T. *Butterfly Host Plants of South-east QLD and Northern New South Wales.* 4th ed. (Butterfly and Other Invertebrates Club, Brisbane, 2019)

Ryan, M. (ed) *Wild Plants of Greater Brisbane.* (Queensland Museum, 2003)

Schwencke, H., Jordan, F. *Butterfly Magic.* (Earthling Enterprises, 1992)

Tallamy, D. W. *Bringing Nature Home: How You Can Sustain Wildlife with Native Plants,* Updated and Expanded. (Timber Press, 2009).

Websites

Insects and other Invertebrates

Australian Butterflies and Moths - https://www.facebook.com/groups/799465170167144

Australian Museum - https://australian.museum/

Amateur Entomology Australia - https://www.facebook.com/groups/AmateurEntomologyAustralia/

Brisbane Insects and Spiders - http://brisbaneinsects.com/pchew_brisbane/index.html

Butterfly and Other Invertebrates Club, Brisbane - boic.org.au, and https://www.facebook.com/groups/187619097411

Butterfly House Coffs Harbour - www.butterflyhouse.com.au

Caterpillars of Butterflies and Moths in Australia - http://lepidoptera.butterflyhouse.com.au/cats.html

Queensland Museum - https://www.qm.qld.gov.au/

Spidentify - https://identify-spiders.com/

[Spiders] - http://www.arachne.org.au/

[Wasps] Australian Polistinae and other Hymenoptera - https://www.facebook.com/groups/188453645581988

What Bug is that? - http://anic.ento.csiro.au/insectfamilies/

Plants

Websites of the nurseries listed in Appendix 3, plus:

Native Plants Queensland - https://www.npq.org.au/

Queensland Bushfood Association - https://qldbushfood.org.au

PlantNET - NSW FloraOnline - https://plantnet.rbgsyd.nsw.gov.au

Queensland Plant Identification - https://www.facebook.com/groups/1590103837875621

Noosa Landcare - https://noosalandcare.org/wp/wp-content/uploads/2019/03/ndlgstocklistsep2020.pdf

Brisbane Rainforest Action and Information Network (BRAIN) - http://www.brisrain.org.au/01_cms/details.asp?ID=9

Nature in general

iNaturalist - https://www.inaturalist.org/

Atlas of Living Australia - https://www.ala.org.au

Queensland Naturalists Club - https://www.qnc.org.au

Questagame - https://questagame.com/

Specialist FB groups - most life-forms have one or more.

Species identification is a highly specialised field for many of the millions and millions of invertebrates, let alone the various species that mimic other species. Be wary of misidentifications, and learn to recognise the features of the different Phyla and their Classes and Orders. Learn to recognise the people who are genuinely knowledgeable.

And this book's publisher: Earthling Enterprises: www.earthling.com.au

About the authors

Helen Schwencke

For over 35 years Helen Schwencke's passion has been connecting people with nature, especially butterflies, native bees and other small creatures (including growing their food sources to increase urban biodiversity). Trained as a biologist/ecologist, Helen was the founding President of the Butterfly and Other Invertebrates Club from 1994 until 2006, and managed Woodfordia's Butterfly (& other invertebrates) Project from 2004 - 2018. Helen is the steward of a 30+ year old, 405sq m inner Brisbane biodiverse 'living laboratory' garden in which she has raised 50 species of butterflies and other invertebrate species, many from eggs to adult, and a further 25 species, mostly from Woodfordia's project. Currently, she is involved in butterfly and invertebrate biodiversity and conservation via presentations, community education programs, displays of her posters of butterfly lifecycles and their host plants called *Butterfly Lives*, and publications such as *Create More Butterflies* (co-author and publisher) and *Australian Stingless Bees* (publisher). Helen is a public speaker, operates an environmental consultancy: Earthling Enterprises (www.earthling.com.au), and enjoys SLOW walking: Seeing, Looking, Observing and Wondering.

Dick Copeman

Dick trained as a doctor and worked in Aboriginal health, community health and general practice for 20 years. He was Senior Lecturer in General Practice at the University of Queensland from 1985 to 1991. He then moved into the arenas of food policy and environmental activism, and in 1994 was a member of the group that founded Northey Street City Farm, a two hectare community garden and orchard in inner Brisbane. Dick initiated permaculture teaching at Northey Street and was the farming team manager there from 2013 to 2016. He is currently coordinator of the city farm's management committee and leader of a volunteer group that looks after the farm's forest gardens and orchards. His interests are in growing plants for food, particularly perennial and tree crops, as well as bush foods, and he teaches regular workshops on these topics. He has also been involved in several long-running bush revegetation projects and is a keen amateur naturalist and bushwalker.

Index

www.ingramcontent.com/pod-product-compliance
Lightning Source LLC
Chambersburg PA
CBHW041259040426
42334CB00028BA/3092